Keys to Living Well

Dharma Words (I)

By
Venerable Master Hsing Yun

Translated by
Venerable Miao Hsi and Cherry Lai

©2005 Buddha's Light Publishing

By Venerable Master Hsing Yun
Translated by Venerable Miao Hsi and Cherry Lai
Edited by Edmond Chang and Robert Smitheram
Book designed by Dung Trieu
Cover designed by Vivian Shih

Published by Buddha's Light Publishing
3456 S. Glenmark Drive,
Hacienda Heights, CA 91745, U.S.A.
Tel: (626) 923-5144
Fax: (626) 923-5145
E-mail: itc@blia.org
Website: www.blpusa.com

ISBN: 1-932293-13-2

Acknowledgments

We received a lot of help from many people and we want to thank them for their efforts in making the publication of this book possible. We especially appreciate Venerable Tzu Jung, the Chief Executive of the Fo Guang Shan International Translation Center (F.G.S.I.T.C.), Venerable Hui Chi, Abbot of Hsi Lai Temple; Venerable Yi Chao for her support and leadership; Venerable Miao Hsi and Cherry Lai for their translation; Edmond Chang and Robert Smitheram for their editing; Venerable Man Jen, Mu-Tzen Hsu, Kevin Hsyeh, and Pey-Rong Lee for proofreading and preparing the manuscript for publication; Vivian Shih for her cover design; and Dung Trieu for her book and cover design. Our appreciation also goes to everyone who has supported this project from its conception to its completion.

CONTENTS

Preface

There are many books and seminars dedicated to giving instruction about how to plan and manage our daily lives. These approaches usually attempt to provide very basic practical suggestions for using time. In the present volume Venerable Master Hsing Yun shares lectures from past presentations as well as new thoughts on his insights about how to plan and live with all the pressures of modern life. He has an approach that is quite different from the many so-called "self help" materials. While it is important to learn certain tasks that save time and make us more efficient, Master Hsing Yun urges people to understand that it is more than rules and ploys that help with planning. The true strategy for dealing with life starts with the understanding that each person has regarding themselves, their situation, and the nature of thought and action. This understanding, from the Buddhist point of view, is necessary for successful change of old habit energy. Unless there are fundamental and insightful developments within our thinking and comprehension, we cannot expect to shift old patterns and permanently leave them behind us. It is this belief that leads Master Hsing Yun to prize learning and commitment to practice as well as to continual striving that leads to transformations of mind and thought.

This volume is filled with very detailed explanations about issues that occupy us from the moment we awake in the morning until the last conscious moment before sleep. The explanations help to frame the problems that are found at every level of activity, whether it is in private or public domains. Having clearly defined the experiences of living, Master Hsing Yun goes on to give concrete advice about how to focus one's thought and avoid the confusion of a mind that is scattered among the many matters that compete for our attention. It is the Buddhist ideal of concentrated attention that can be a solution to all of us who live and work in the world of freeways, computers, telephones, radios, faxes, email, and encounters with other people. While the external environment can be chaotic and demanding, it is possible for individuals to practice concentration, which permits purposeful action. Mere rules and programming methods of dealing with problems can never solve the complex constantly changing situations in which we find ourselves. Every moment brings a new assault on our sensory domain, new and unexpected matters sweep across our mental and physical horizons. Methods that are built on the assumption that there are a limited set of variables, fail miserably in a world that exhibits flux and flow of constant change. It is impossible to create a list of items that can be guaranteed to solve any potential problem in the future. Master Hsing Yun tells his audiences that only when one has created a mind that is flexible and concentrated can we hope to cope with the rush and force of every moment.

Achieving the state of being calm and composed in the face of any event can come from long and continued efforts of focused thought and exposure to the teachings of Buddhist sages. It is in this manner that the Buddhist community becomes an important part of life. Through the community, Buddhists receive support in the form of teaching and practice. One of the facets of Humanistic Buddhism is to take the principles of the teaching and apply them to the world around us. While there is need for inner development, concentrated thought, and calmness of spirit, the outer expression of the wisdom gained must find its place among others.

All of this, and more, is given in the elegant teaching style of the Master. He leads us from one perspective to another in understandable and challenging ways. For any individual who wants to have more control over time, work, and obligations, this volume offers a deep and long-lasting solution.

Lewis Lancaster
President
University of the West

Keys to Living Well

Dharma Words (1)

One Day to a Lifetime

With the advancements in technology, people today emphasize convenience and comfort in life. They become complacent and avoid hard work, and as a result, they often waste precious time. A Ming Dynasty poet, Tang Bohu, once wrote, "It is rare for someone to live seventy years. If you take away the years of childhood and old age, not much time is left in between. Then there are the hot and cold seasons as well as so many worries to take into account." In our life, after discounting time for sleep, sickness, old age, and childhood, how much is actually left for us to use? Therefore, we should make good use of our limited life span and plan well. We should start by carefully planning "one day to a lifetime," living each day as if it were a hundred years so that we can contribute fully to the world. The following are keys for planning "one day to a lifetime."

1. Plans for the day start in the morning. Each morning, we should plan what we have to complete for the day. When we have plans and goals, the day will not be wasted. Napoleon once said, "If I let a day go by without doing anything meaningful, I feel like I have committed theft." If we do not plan well for the day, not only will we feel stressed and unprepared in dealing with matters, but we also may forget or neglect what is important. We will end up wasting time just letting things go by. The poet Tao Yuanming cautioned, "The prime years of life will not come again, and there will not be another dawning of this day." If we do not plan well in the morning, we are simply "allowing our youthful hair to turn gray and feeling sorrow for nothing gained."

2. Plans for everything start with having a clear mind. Confucius said, "The wise are without delusions."

Someone with wisdom can discern right from wrong and is clear from beginning to end about any matter. When we come across special cases or urgent matters regarding personnel at work, it is very important for us to understand the fundamental issue in order to find solutions for these problems. If we can truly appreciate the truth and the priorities of everything, we can make the right decision. We must be clear about every matter and have correct views in order to avoid making mistakes. Plans for everything, therefore, must start with having a clear mind.

3. Plans for a family start with peace and harmony. Members of the same family will inevitably be different. Respect, appreciation, and support for one another are ways to achieve peace and harmony. A popular saying reminds us, "A harmonious family prospers in everything." The peace and harmony of the family directly affects the spiritual and mental development of its members. It also influences human relationships with others and even social stability. Zhu Xi, a Song Dynasty philosopher once said, "Etiquette is fundamental for preserving a family; harmony is fundamental for bringing prosperity to the family." Families are the roots of a society, while peace and harmony are the foundations of a family. Therefore plans for a family must start with peace and harmony.

4. Plans for a lifetime start with diligence. The most important word in life is diligence. Isaac Newton once said, "If you want to acquire knowledge, food, and happiness, you must work hard because diligence is the cardinal rule for gaining everything." As long as we work hard, we can certainly excel in what we are learning and create a career of outstanding success. On the other hand, if we are lazy, we will lose what we have. Even though we

may have great ambition, nothing can come to fruition without hard work. *The Yan Family Precepts* states, "One out of ten people in the world give up because of difficulty; nine out of ten people in the world give up because of laziness." Therefore, there is rarely insurmountable difficulty in the world, for as long as we are diligent, we can surely succeed.

Our life should be constantly renewed, especially in making changes to our mind and body. We must know how to plan our lives well. We need to make plans for a day, a month, a year, and a lifetime, as well as be willing to make vows.

A Day's Life

How do you live your life every day? Is there any planning? During the time of the *Spring and Autumn Annals*, the prime minister of the Qi Kingdom, Guan Zhong said, "Planning for a year is like developing a valley; planning for ten years is like planting trees, and planning for a lifetime is like educating a person." Therefore, each of us should make plans for one year, ten years, and a lifetime. Moreover, the most important thing to do is to plan our everyday life so that time will not be wasted.

While there will inevitably be unforeseen or unexpected incidents from day to day, we still need to make plans for our daily life and work. How do we plan for our everyday life? The following are four points for consideration:

1. Think in the morning. In *The Great Learning* [*Da Xue*], it is said, "Things have their root and their branches. Affairs have their end and their beginning. To know what is first and what is last will bring one closer to the Way." Morning is when our mind is clearest. We can think or write in our notebook the things we have to complete that day and make plans to finish them. For instance, we may have to write letters to friends, fulfill what others ask us to do, or complete the jobs our supervisors want us to finish. Planning ahead, we will not forget responsibilities or make mistakes in our day's work.

2. Act during the day. The ancients said, "Don't put off till tomorrow what can be done today. Don't pass on to others what you can do yourself." The day starts after breakfast when our work should begin. We need to actively make progress every day and diligently apply ourselves to complete all the things we plan to do within the day.

3. Reflect in the evening. When evening comes, we should cultivate the habit of self-reflection. "What are the merits I have achieved today? What are the faults?" Yuan Liaofan, a dedicated practitioner from the Ming Dynasty, had the habit of recording his merits and faults every day. Zengzi, a disciple of Confucius, reflected daily, "Am I loyal in working for others? Am I trustworthy in dealing with my friends? Do I put into practice what I teach others?" It is very important to perform this self-reflection every evening because by reviewing our daily actions and speech over time, we can be certain that our life will improve, our morals will increase, and our character will reach a higher level.

4. Rest at night. Night is the time to rest and sleep. We should not be socializing, for if we exhaust our energy and spirit living such a topsy-turvy life, we will be worn-out in no time. We will not have the energy to face life the next day. Therefore, proper rest is necessary for going further on our path.

We must know how to plan each day as we live in the hustle and bustle of today's society. We need to follow these four points every day in order to have a meaningful life.

Beginnings

The origin of all our behavior derives from how we think. Therefore, each thought in our mind is the beginning of whether we rise to heaven or sink into hell. Our every thought creates the result of either being in the world of the Buddha or in one of suffering. Therefore, we must be cautious about how we begin. Whether a beginning is good or bad, right or wrong, will determine success or failure in the future. The following explanations describe the importance of beginnings.

1. Lofty mountains and steep ridges begin with earth mounds. They were not always lofty and steep. They may even have been transformed originally from oceans into fields, then changed into earth mounds and hills, and gradually developed into mountain ranges. Unwholesome behavior also starts from small deeds, growing serious over time, and a devious criminal may start out with just a negative thought. As such, we must be wary of our first thought on any matter. Liu Bei, the ruler of the Shu Kingdom during the Period of the Three Kingdoms, advised, "Do not refrain from doing a small act of kindness nor commit a small act of evil just because it is small." We must be aware of ourselves at all times so that our unwholesome thoughts will not accumulate. Diligent self-reflection will prevent our self-destruction.

2. Vast oceans begin with small streams. It is said in the *Sutra on the Treasury of Truth* [*Dharmapada Sutra*], "Water drops may be small, but they can gradually fill a large container." Small streams can accumulate to form a Yangzi or a Yellow River over time, and even become a large ocean. Therefore, we cannot afford to belittle

small streams. The Western Jin Dynasty scholar Lu Ji said, "Do not overlook small acts in creating long-term results; do not rely on only major deeds in establishing merit." A small act of kindness may save someone's life and a minor connection we make may change the life of another. Therefore, even small gestures of kindness can eventually lead to immense merit.

3. Millennia and kalpas begin with a moment. A thousand years or ten thousand kalpas seem to be a very long time. However, they all begin in a moment or a split second, and build up gradually. Similarly, successful entrepreneurs, creative designers, famous writers, and others who have acquired celebrity status in society, have all gradually cultivated their wisdom, creativity, skills, and expertise over time. They have passed the test of time and gained experience through their efforts. No single matter in the world arises from nothing. Success is only achieved through the process of learning and passing the test of time.

4. Attaining the Way begins with faith. People who attain spiritual enlightenment or success in society all rely on their firm faith in what is essential and true. Because they hold onto what they have learned, and maintain the right faith in the goals they establish, they can achieve tremendous success. The *Flower Adornment Sutra* [*Avatamsaka Sutra*] teaches, "Faith and confidence can enhance wisdom. With faith we can reach the state of the Buddha." The *Treatise on the Perfection of Great Wisdom* [*Mahaprajnaparamita Sastra*] also says, "Faith is like the hands of a person. When one arrives at a mountain of treasure, one can freely pick up the treasure only if one has hands. Otherwise, nothing can be gained." Therefore, faith is the foundation of learning and cultivating the Way.

According to a popular saying, "A good beginning is half of the way to success." If our direction is right when we start out, we can certainly reach our destination; when our thought is right at the beginning, our behavior will not go wrong. The beginning of every action is very important. Therefore, we must always pay close attention to how we begin.

How to Manage Ourselves

People today emphasize planning, organization, and management in everything they do. For instance, our careers, families, and human relationships all need management. In addition, those who are wise work to enhance social welfare and culture; those who are benevolent work to enhance charity and righteousness; those who are respectful work to enhance finances and friends; and those who are enthusiastic practitioners work to enhance happiness and Dharma joy. However, ultimately, people need to know how to manage themselves as individuals. Here are four keys for self-management:

1. Seek improvement in learning. Life is a path of endless learning. A saying reminds us, "Learning is never complete, for you are never too old to learn." Learning is not temporary; it is a lifelong endeavor, and it is not limited either to what happens at school. There is always something to learn within a household, company, or community. In fact, society in general is like a university providing us with endless opportunities for learning. When learning, it is most important to strive for improvement. We should not be complacent or arrogant, because by always seeking to improve we will be able to raise ourselves to a higher level.

2. Venture wide and deep in the industrial and commercial worlds. These are times of advanced communication and active industrial and commercial development. After graduating from school, we all need to join the workforce. Whether it be in commerce, industry or agriculture, there are various organizations, such as cooperatives, unions and farmers' associations, that exemplify how teamwork and human interactions are emphasized in

today's world. So when we participate in a meeting and associate with other people, we need to pay attention to all levels of relationships. Only when we can appreciate and manage human relationships on multiple levels, will we be able to venture wider and deeper in our careers, and succeed more easily in what we do.

3. Be cheerful in managing human relationships. No one can live life shut off from the rest of the world, especially in our modern society where human interaction is dynamic and ubiquitous. People today are closely linked with the societies, the world, the earth and even the universe, in which they live. Thus, we need to know how to manage human relationships well. We should give others joy and benefit. In developing our careers, we must be cheerful and able to share a laugh with others. We need to have a sense of humor and not be stiff or solemn, so as to gain the support of others.

4. Be calm and connect with our spiritual side when we are alone. Keeping busy and being tense is often the portrait of a modern life. When we are alone by ourselves at night after a day of hustle and bustle at the workplace, we should not be thinking about the right and wrong between self and others experienced during the day; and we should not be obsessing about the good or bad nor the loss or gain of our work. Instead, we should calm ourselves to enjoy the peace of our mind and our spiritual world in order to gain strength to start the next day refreshed.

A very successful Japanese entrepreneur, Konosuke Matsushita, was praised as "a god of management." Aside from his outstanding business success and personal wealth, he also gained recognition for his humanistic style of leadership, which was the true basis of his success. Therefore, in life, we not only need to manage our tangible wealth well. More importantly, we must also learn to manage our intangible spiritual world. This is indeed the key to good self-management.

Life's Driving Forces

Horses and cattle subsist on grass and hay to gain strength to carry heavy loads and travel long distances. In addition to eating three meals a day, humans also need constant spiritual reinforcement in order to have the strength to move on in life. There are six driving forces in life for us to consider:

1. Plant seeds of compassion in place of anger and hatred. Anger, hatred, and confrontation create mountains between self and others, as well as place obstacles in our paths. The more others take us as their enemy, treat us poorly or hate us, the more we need to plant seeds of compassion, because only compassion can dissolve hatred and anger. We should never add fuel to the flames of hatred by being hateful and angry ourselves. Otherwise, when will the cycle of mutual enmity end? Moreover, Dharma practitioners should not find enemies in others. The greatest enemy is always oneself. But if we really have an enemy in our heart, we should make the best effort to love him or her. This is the greatest driving force for self-improvement. Therefore, we need to always plant seeds of compassion to eradicate hatred.

2. Be forgiving and understanding instead of holding any grudges. We must never allow a grudge to fester and grow inside our mind, because we will only be harming ourselves in the end. The greatest virtue in life is forgiveness. When there is animosity from others, we need to be forgiving and understanding. We should not be calculating and attached to our views. Therefore, we need forgiveness and understanding to overcome animosity and the holding of grudges.

3. Cultivate the strength of confidence in place of suspi-

cion. "A suspicious heart breeds the ghosts of darkness." When we have suspicions, we need to cultivate self-confidence. When others are suspicious of us, we also need to inspire them with confidence. With confidence, there will be strength to help us solve problems.

4. Light the fire of prajna-wisdom in place of darkness. "A room dark for a thousand years can be lit up with only a single lamp." Light signifies wisdom. No matter how ignorant and deluded a person is, when prajna-wisdom is developed, it is like a light that chases away darkness. Therefore, when misunderstanding begins to affect our human relationships or when we are feeling low and frustrated, we need to light the fire of prajna-wisdom to solve problems, and never allow anger to rule us.

5. Raise hope for the future in times of disappointment. When others are disheartened and disappointed, we need to encourage and comfort them, giving them hope for the future. We should let them believe tomorrow will be a better day, and the future more promising. It is a supreme gift to make people feel that their future is full of hope.

6. Provide the comfort of joy in times of sorrow. When people are suffering and frustrated, if we help them with their problems and bring them joy, we will win their trust and friendship.

People need to learn how to transform their minds and change their ways. Transforming minds and overcoming unwholesome habits are the driving forces for self-improvement. Furthermore, self-reflection is the driving force behind success; confidence is the driving force for reaching our goals; compassion is the driving force for a harmonious family; and selflessness is the greatest driving force for peace in the universe. Moreover, whenever we interact with others, we should also use our compassion, wisdom, tolerance, and confidence to help others activate their own driving forces in life.

The Four Minds in Life

There are many qualities of mind: defiled or pure, biased or unbiased, deluded or awakened. The mind can also be distinguished as deluded or true. The deluded mind is polluted, discriminating, and disordered. The true mind, on the other hand, is a mind of loving-kindness, compassion, joy, and equanimity—the Four Immeasurables. These four qualities not only generate merit and wisdom, but also benefit all sentient beings. The following is how we can use the Four Immeasurables as the foundation for conducting ourselves in society.

1. Approach the world with loving-kindness. We should have a loving heart so that we can get along with people and deal with matters. Having a loving heart is giving others joy and ease. In addition, it means having understanding, being forgiving, and being willing to serve others. When we have a loving heart, we will be tolerant and not commit impulsive acts that will be disadvantageous to others. In *The Great Learning*, it is said, "Rely on ultimate kindness." This implies we should benefit all sentient beings with a loving heart, and practice social welfare with pure kindness in order to benefit humanity.

2. Help people with compassion. People should have compassion for the universe. Compassion gives us the capacity to uproot the suffering of others and offer them joy. It is the heart of Avalokitesvara Bodhisattva, which relieves the suffering and overcomes the difficulties of sentient beings. In helping others, we need true compassion so that we will not care about our own gains and losses. Also, we should not discriminate among people according to their social status or differentiate people as friend or foe. We should help all with an unbiased mind

like the sun shining on the world universally without expecting anything in return. Therefore, we must have compassion in helping others so that we can be truly selfless in providing them with assistance.

3. Work with joy in your heart. Do you feel joy as you work every day? Or, do you feel regret and unhappiness about what you do? In work, we need to be "perfectly willing" so that we can be happy. Only when we have a heart of joy in getting along with others and dealing with matters will others feel our sincerity. However, if we are unhappy with our work, we will get tired easily and find everything difficult to do. But if we have joy in our hearts, others will also feel happy too, and then no matter how much work there is, no one will feel tired. For thirty years, a monk by the name of Tuobiao who lived during the Buddha's time carried a heart of joy with his lantern in showing guests of his monastery to their rooms at night. In doing so, he benefited both himself and others.

4. Practice with equanimity. Do you wish to practice Buddhism? Do you like to cultivate your body and nurture your mind? Practice and cultivation all require a mind of equanimity. With a mind of equanimity, we will be able to let go, see beyond every matter, and not become calculating or attached to the self. Cultivating ourselves also requires letting go of our unwholesome habits and unkind behaviors. According to an old saying, "we can only gain by giving." If we often take the initiative to give others a smile or to help them in some way, we will obtain more positive responses.

The Four Immeasurables–loving-kindness, compassion, joy, and equanimity–are the four spiritual aspects that bodhisattvas embody in providing universal benefit to all sentient beings. They are also the four qualities of mind people should cultivate in life.

The Fundamentals of Being Human

Trees have roots so they can grow and survive. People need a foundation in order to learn the Way and be the master of their lives. Based on the saying, "With a firm foundation, the Way will develop," Venerable Master Huineng elaborated in the *Platform Sutra of the Sixth Patriarch* [*Liuzu Tan Jing*], "Without knowing the essential mind, learning the Dharma is of no benefit." So, what is the essential foundation of humanity? The following are the four fundamentals of being human:

1. Love and filial piety are fundamental between parents and children. The parent-child relationship is the focus of today's society. We emphasize parents nurturing and loving their children, and children respecting and showing filial piety towards their parents. If the older generation in the family does not love and the younger generation does not show respect, then the basic family relationship will lose its ethical order, and the family will lose its foundation. Family members will then find it difficult to live in harmony or remain healthy. Therefore, loving parents and respectful children are fundamental to a household's peace and joy.

2. Mutual respect and love are fundamental between spouses. When a man and a woman marry to form a family, they should respect and love one another. They should not fight or blame each other all the time. There is a Chinese saying, "If one is not from the same family, then one will not enter the doors of the same house." Since spouses choose to be of the same family, then love should be their foundation. This means they should be loving and respectful of each other, as well as offer each other mutual support, understanding, and consideration.

Being devoted, loving, and sincere towards one another is fundamental between spouses.

3. Humility and courtesy are fundamental between seniors and juniors. Some families may be very large with many siblings, and even include such extended family members as uncles, aunts, and cousins. How should they get along? The most important thing is to maintain a proper order between seniors and juniors. When seniors are amiable and juniors are courteous, they will be able to get along. Humility and courtesy are thus fundamental to human ethics. If a family has no order regarding seniority, with seniors not being respected and juniors not being supported and protected, or even worse, the juniors are disrespectful to the seniors, then a peaceful family life will be difficult to maintain.

4. Trust and righteousness are fundamental between friends. Being human is special because we have a sense of reason and righteousness. It is said, "Do not say words that are false; do not befriend people who lack righteousness." In making friends, we should base the friendship on trust and righteousness and not on money or materialism. If friends are only good for fun and good times, such friendships will not last. True friends emphasize trustworthiness and righteousness, because only friendships based on these qualities can last over time.

"Water has its fountainhead and trees have their roots." With a fountainhead, water can flow on and on; with roots, trees can grow strong and tall. Therefore, we have to work on our fundamentals in any given matter, for we cannot put the cart before the horse in whatever we do. We should never forget our fundamentals, because only when we have a firm foundation, can we expand our life.

How to Benefit Ourselves

When a cup can be filled with something to drink, it is functioning properly. When people can accept advice, they can enhance their morals and are worthy of major responsibility. For any matter, we need to be accepting before it can be beneficial to us. If we keep rejecting everything, nothing can enter our mind and benefit us. Many people can reap benefits for a lifetime just by listening to a Dharma verse or maxim. Better still, it is not just for their own benefit, but others will gain as well. So whether we are busy or just relaxing, on the go or at rest, we should have an accepting heart, always being receptive like an empty vessel. By accepting what is beneficial, we can turn it into nourishment for ourselves, for we should not insulate ourselves by rejecting everything because that would mean being unable to benefit from anything.

How can we benefit ourselves? *Humble Table, Wise Fare* offers the following four suggestions for our consideration:

1. Not wasting time in leisure, one will benefit when busy. A person's success often hinges on charging ahead at the crucial moment, and bringing his or her abilities into full play in order to accomplish a task. Yet, we should not overlook the importance of developing depth and substance, as well as cultivating positive conditions on a regular basis. Therefore, even when we are relaxing, we should not slack off. We must also make plans for leisure time, taking advantage of the opportunity to go deep in our cultivation and gather force for the future. Since ancient times, sages and worthies have known how to conceal their abilities, biding their time and waiting for the right causes and conditions to appear. Therefore, we should replenish our energy and resources during quiet

times in order to be ready to charge ahead when the opportunity arises.

2. Not acting unconscionably when alone, one will benefit when in public. This is an age of transparency, when many matters have to pass the test of others' scrutiny and be open, fair, and just. They need to withstand the glare of the sun, so as to show there is nothing to hide. Actually, even in ancient times, there was a teaching, that "the gentleman is cautious in a dark room." An inferior person will do unwholesome things when alone, but an ethical person is vigilant of his or her morals even when alone. We should always exercise self-restraint and self-discipline as if there were "ten pairs of eyes watching and ten pair of hands admonishing us." We should develop the capacity to say, "There is no book I have not read; there is nothing I cannot speak of." Once the open-mindedness to discuss any matter with others has become a habit, we will be able to conduct ourselves in an upright manner, acting the same whether in public or private. In this way, we will earn the respect of others. So when we act in good conscience even when alone, we will naturally benefit when we are with others.

3. Not moving rashly when at rest, one will benefit when in motion. "The universe is great in its motion; the days are long in quietude." Life entails both action and inaction. When we are in action, we should be lively and full of energy, integrating with society in order to fully develop ourselves. When we are at rest, we should learn to enjoy peace and tranquility, and appreciate the carefree leisure of being by ourselves. Thus, not moving rashly when at rest, we can benefit when in motion. Once we know how to cultivate our strengths when passive, we can begin again at any time. Therefore, we should be both active and passive in life. When we can embody both action and inaction, we will have the best approach to life.

4. Not being attached when deluded, one will benefit when awakened. When we are deluded, we often have many worries knotted in our hearts. Most of the time, it is the result of our obsessions and attachments to our views, which prevent us from accepting the wise counsel of others. So when you feel things are not going well and are plagued with worries, no matter how much delusion, ignorance, and wrong view trouble you, as long as you can remain unattached to them, there will always be a solution. As the saying goes, "Exhausting all possibilities brings change and change brings success." When we keep searching for solutions, we will reach a realization, and as long as there is realization, we will benefit. This is the meaning of "not being attached when deluded, one will benefit when awakened."

When Buddhism discusses enlightenment, it makes the distinction between sudden and gradual realization. But even "sudden" realization must be achieved through a gradual cultivation over time. In our learning process, whether or not we can keep progressing depends on how we apply our mind. If we can pay attention everywhere we go, be humble all the time, and not give up on the small details, then over time, little by little, we will certainly benefit from our cultivation as it matures.

The Wonderful Ways of Keeping Busy

Being busy characterizes the lifestyle of people in today's society. They are busy at work, taking care of the family, managing their finances, studying for exams, socializing with friends, chatting on the Internet, meeting deadlines, following the stock market, shopping in malls, visiting each other's homes. No matter what we may be busy with, as long as there is fun, meaning, and value, there can be endless wonders in keeping busy.

So what are the wonderful ways of keeping busy? Here are four possibilities:

1. There should be Dharma joy in keeping busy. In life, we are either busy or idle. Some of us take joy in keeping busy, because it offers us the opportunity to learn and mature. Being busy enriches our lives, for in keeping our body and mind occupied, we can gain a sense of achievement from our work, as well as gain confidence in our abilities. More importantly, there's a saying that "Busy people have no illusions." Without illusions, we can naturally be at peace and happy. Therefore, when we feel joy in keeping busy, we will not suffer or get lazy. If we enjoy being busy, we will be perfectly willing to keep at it.

2. There should be meaning in keeping busy. Keeping busy is nourishment. It can enhance our spiritual health, cultivate good causes and conditions, bring our life force into full play, and elevate the value of life. However, some people are only busy indulging themselves in drinking and eating all day. Keeping busy with such mundane pleasures not only wastes money, but also affects our health. We should instead keep busy by doing things that benefit our health, enhance our morals, inspire our wisdom, and cultivate meaningful human

connections. Only in this way, then, can keeping busy become meaningful.

3. There should be efficiency in keeping busy. "With a division of work, there will be no need to rush; with planning, there will be no chaos." The worst thing for us would be to try and do everything ourselves. When we do not know how to allocate and distribute responsibilities at work, we cannot cooperate with others, and thus, we become inefficient. Many people are unorganized in their work. Without any planning, they blindly rush about keeping busy without a clear direction or purpose. Efficiency is of great importance in whatever we do. Besides organizing our work, we also need to simplify matters, and if necessary, replace labor with other resources. What is most important is following up on the results. An hour's work should produce an hour's result. The same goes for a day's, a week's or a month's work. When we can plan well ahead of time and follow up on the results, then there will be efficiency in our work as we keep busy.

4. There should be value in keeping busy. Keeping busy is an important path to follow. However, some people keep themselves busy all day only for their own status and wealth. Others may be working to provide three meals a day for their families. Yet, there are those who strive to benefit society, and even those who fly around the globe promoting world peace. Keeping busy should, therefore, not be just for our own benefit. We should also work for the welfare of our family, country, society, and especially for all of humanity, so that our efforts will become more valuable.

The more we work, the more we can do; the busier we are, the more we can handle being busy. Keeping busy is like a sharp sword that can cut through the veil of illusion. It can transform decay into wonder, and like wholesome food, it can nourish our body. Keeping busy can fill our lives with endless opportunities.

The Use of "One"

Between "one" and "many," people naturally assume "many" is better. In reality, "many" is not necessarily good, while "one" can sometimes work wonders. The story below illustrates this.

There were two men traveling together. One had a necklace with a pendant of Avalokitesvara Bodhisattva, and the other carried with him a good number of portraits of deities and gods. Suddenly, a robber descended on them. As the robber wielded a big knife and lunged at them, the man wearing only the Avalokitesvara Bodhisattva pendant was not hurt. The necklace he was wearing absorbed the blow and became twisted. He was very grateful to the Bodhisattva for protecting him from danger. However, the other man carrying many icons had his arm chopped off. He was angry and complained, "How come with the many gods and deities that I believe in, none of them came to save me, while the man with only Avalokitesvara Bodhisattva as his guardian was spared?" At that time, the many gods and deities spoke to him, "We're sorry! Because there are so many gods and deities, it would have been rude if any of us just stepped forward without consensus. We started out sending an earth deity to save you, but he was too embarrassed to act on his own. So he sent Laozi who in turn asked Jesus. Jesus then went to Mohammed for help. As we were trying to decide who would go, the robber came down with his knife and injured you."

From the above story, we can see the reliable use of "one." A person's faith should never be too complicated. It needs to be simple. Even Buddhism teaches, "No water will end up being drawn if three monks are sent." Therefore, it is best to be single-minded. There are four points regarding the use of "one":

1. One instance of patience can counter a hundred acts of

courage. We need to be brave in life. However, we cannot rely on courage alone in what we do. "Lack of patience in small matters spoils great undertakings." When we only have courage and no wisdom, we cannot succeed. We should emulate those with patience who can remain calm before challenges. "Being calm, we can think clearly; thinking clearly, we can accomplish things." This is how one instance of patience can help us succeed and counter a hundred acts of courage.

2. One moment of tranquility can overcome a hundred actions. When warriors test their skills or masters duel, they need to overcome action with calmness. When opposing armies battle, if intelligence is unclear, it is better to remain stationary than to make a rash move. "Being calm, we can go far." "Being idle, we can ponder how to move." When we are calm and quiet, we can observe the entire situation, and we will not make any false moves that may bring us trouble.

3. One act of diligence can accomplish a hundred deeds. Confucianism teaches, "Diligence accomplishes, while frolic ruins a career" and "Nothing is difficult when diligence is applied." Buddhism teaches the "Four Right Types of Diligence." It tells us that, "If one is lazy as a layperson, one loses in worldly gains; if one is lazy as a monastic, one loses the right Dharma." Diligence is indeed important as it can make up for our shortcomings. As long as we are willing to work hard, it does not matter if we are wise or foolish, we can certainly develop a fulfilling career.

4. One benevolent deed can eradicate a hundred evils. The sutra says, "One kind thought is sufficient for attaining Buddhahood." The kind thought of a young novice monk to save a colony of drowning ants ended up adding years to his short life. A benevolent deed can outweigh much unwholesome karma. Therefore, we should never

underestimate a single benevolent or harmful thought. Instead, we should be very aware of our every thought and be able to always keep kindness and compassion on our mind. In doing so, we can naturally eradicate much unwholesome karma in our life.

Buddhism teaches, "the practice of non-duality," "the universe within one thought," and "one is all." The use of "one" is surely infinite.

Between Self and Others

If we want to elevate ourselves in life, we need an education of ideas as a source of inspiration. In dealing with self and others, it takes an education of life to train us. The following are four points about how to interact well with others:

1. Saying too much is cheapening our precious life. As the saying goes, "Too much glue does not stick well; too many words are unpleasant." When speaking, the intention is to express ourselves and convey ideas. We should be concise and never be wordy. However, while something can be conveyed in a few short sentences, some people choose to repeat themselves over and over again. A public lecture which should only take thirty minutes to an hour may last two or three if the speaker drags on. In saying too much, not only do others get tired of us, but we also waste precious life. Therefore, we do not need to say too much. Words are only valuable if they benefit others.

2. Unnecessary socializing is a waste of valuable time. Socializing and networking are to some degree inevitable in today's world. While some socializing is necessary, most occasions are just a waste of time. How much time is there in life for us to use? Some people simply do not cherish their time, and often waste it on unnecessary and meaningless social engagements that benefit no one. Too much socializing is therefore truly regrettable.

3. Being alone is the best opportunity for self-cultivation. In getting along with others, the sound of applause is important to share. However, when alone, sometimes it is better for there to be no sound at all. Therefore, while we need to live within a group during the day, we should

also find time to be alone by ourselves. "Being alone" is for contemplation of our internal world. We need to look within ourselves for a formless world and listen for soundless sound. Whenever we are alone, we should not just read the newspapers, watch television, or listen to music. Such popular media are still full of gossip and idle talk that prevent us from staying calm and serene. Being alone gives us relief from thinking, watching, or listening, so that we can discover our true self.

4. Being gregarious is a force for motivating others. While a person can be calm, one also needs to move and extend beyond one's personal boundaries. Even though a person can be alone, one also needs to be gregarious. People who can mingle with a group can assimilate well into society. They are able to get along with others, work as a team, contribute their energy and spirit, and serve the community. They become the force behind social progress. Therefore, being gregarious is a force for motivating others. As the saying goes, "Arrogant people find it hard to form friendships with others; selfish people have difficulty gaining support from a group."

In getting along with others, we should be pliable and yielding like water. We should be especially mindful of others and considerate of their needs at all times.

How to Get Along in a Group

Nobody is an island and no one can survive all alone. Getting along with others within a group is an art as well as a form of cultivation. Therefore, we not only need to understand human nature, but we must also pay special attention to the moral standards for communal living so that others will not reject us. The following six points are suggestions on how to improve relations with others in a group:

1. Treat others with a kind heart. There is a saying, "A good heart bears good fruit." However, sometimes people may not accept our kindheartedness. We should not lose faith because time is the best test: as long as we are sincere and consistent in treating others with kindness, the day will come when they will reciprocate. Therefore, a kind heart bears good fruit because the Law of Cause and Effect will not let us down.

2. Win over others with virtue. "Birds flock to high mountains; people are drawn to noble virtues." If we try to pressure people with power, our efforts will fail. We may be very knowledgeable and learned, but others may still not need us. However, if we have virtue, compassion, sincerity, and integrity, others will come to have trust in us. It is said, "In using power to cower others, troubles will not be far off. In using morality to influence others, a good reputation will last far and long." When we use virtue to win over others, they will respond favorably. Therefore, the wise cultivate morality and the petty power.

3. Move others with genuine feelings. "When feelings are genuine, friendships will run deep." When we are deeply compassionate and caring, truly helping and supporting

others in their endeavors, our genuine feelings will be evident in our actions. Gradually, people around us will be moved by what we do, and those far away will also be drawn to us. It is because we are sincere in our feelings, that even a rock can be moved, not to speak of humans, the most sentient form of living beings.

4. Counsel others with sincerity. Sincerity is the most valuable quality in a person. True sincerity can even move a heart of stone. When others have erred, we should offer our advice with calm equanimity. But even as we convey our advice with clarity, it is even more important to convey it with sincerity. Through our sincerity, we will gain the confidence and trust of others. According to a saying, "If we want good human relations, we should be sincere and not arrogant." Sincerity is of great benefit to self and others.

5. Greet others with a smile. A smile is the sunshine of human relationships. Whenever we meet someone, a smile should be the first thing we offer. A smile can free people from worries and console those in sorrow. What is the most beautiful thing in the world? It is a smile, because the easiest way to connect with someone is through a smile. Sometimes, a warm smile or a good laugh will sweep away all misunderstandings and unhappiness. Therefore, we should always greet people with a smiling face and beautify life with smiles.

6. Love others with compassion. People are supreme because of their capacity for compassion, loving-kindness, joy, and equanimity. Compassion is the greatest virtue in life. The problems people have can be resolved with wisdom. The tension between people, however, can only be eradicated with compassion. When we need to counsel someone, compassionate words and gestures along with a caring heart are most effective. Compassion is the common wealth we share with all sen-

tient beings. "Of the many paths of goodness, compassion is the most expedient." Compassion is vowing to fulfill ourselves by helping others succeed. Therefore, being compassionate to others, we can sow good conditions for ourselves, and loving others with compassion, we can attain harmony with others.

To assure a future we can look forward to, we need to establish harmonious relationships. We need to take the initiative to care for others, for we can only truly exist when we are aware of the existence of others.

How to Make Connections

Buddhism often speaks about cause and effect. For a cause to lead to an effect, there is something very important in between: conditions. Conditions are a strength that enhances and nourishes. When a seed is planted in the soil, it must have sunshine, air, and water as supporting conditions before it can blossom and bear fruit. "Conditions" are an important quality bringing a cause into an effect. Therefore, if we want to establish ourselves and succeed in life, we must make use of every opportunity to create positive conditions by making connections with people. The following four points are keys on how to make connections:

1. We must be thankful for past causes and conditions. Without past causes and conditions, there would not be the present effect. For instance, our parents are our past causes and conditions. They gave us life and nourished us. We should honor and love them in repayment for what they have done for us. Moreover, our teachers teach us, friends and relatives encourage us, our country protects us, and the different professions of society support us. We need to be thankful for all of these past causes and conditions so we can repay them appropriately. Much of the social chaos today results from people failing to be grateful for their past causes and conditions. They take everything for granted. Not only do they not give thanks, but they are also filled with complaints and dissatisfaction resulting in endless conflict.

2. We must cherish the present causes and conditions. The *Lotus Sutra* says, "The human body is difficult to attain"; it is like "a blind turtle seeking a floating ring in the ocean." *The Discourses of the Buddha* also states, "The opportunity to gain human form is as small as the dirt in

our nails; the opportunity for losing it is as abundant as the soil of the earth." The human realm determines our rise or fall. Because human life is filled with both joy and suffering, it is best for cultivation. This is why the Buddhas of the past, present, and future all attain Buddhahood in the human realm. Our being born as human beings is truly a rare opportunity. We should treasure this cause and condition by actively striving to improve our lives and make positive progress. As long as we cherish our causes and conditions, whatever we do can be sustained over time. In so cherishing we make our lives more extensive and more fulfilling.

3. We must make good use of the causes and conditions in the here and now. Opportunities in life are uncertain; they come and go fleetingly. We must therefore make good use of all the positive causes and conditions we encounter at every moment. Moreover, no matter how smooth or difficult, how beneficial or harmful, these causes and conditions become, as long as we have the Dharma, we can transform them into positive conditions to put us on the bodhi (enlightenment) path to realization. For instance, while spring breezes and summer rains sustain all things, autumn frost and winter snow also help nurture them to fruition. Without being blown by winds and baked by the sun, pineapples will not ripen. Therefore, we should not fear difficulties and setbacks, because without difficulties, our wisdom will not develop, and without setbacks, our resolve will not be firm. A person who makes good use of the causes and conditions in the here and now will attain greater accomplishments much faster than others.

4. We must cultivate future causes and conditions. The most beautiful thing in life is making connections and creating affinities with others. It is said, "Before attaining Buddhahood, we need to make connections with peo-

ple." When some people face difficulties, they often obtain timely help from benefactors. This is the result of their having cultivated causes and conditions in the past. Therefore, the connections we make today are preparation for future difficulties. In our everyday life, by saying a few good words, giving others some support, showing them respect, and having joy in our hearts, we are able to cultivate wonderful and sometimes incredible causes and conditions with others for the future.

There are conditions close at hand and far away; some we can see, and others we cannot. So in order to always assure favorable causes and conditions, we should be thankful for those in the past, cherish those in the present, make good use of those in the here and now, and actively cultivate those in the future.

How to Conduct Ourselves

We often hear people lament, "It is so difficult to conduct oneself properly." Actually, it is not that hard. The difficulty lies in whether we are willing to accept our disadvantages and serve others. But if we are considerate of others, know what we can and cannot do, teach people what we know, and establish good interpersonal relationships, then where is the difficulty? If we know how to conduct ourselves properly, life will be filled with happiness. The following are four suggestions on how to conduct ourselves:

1. Be someone who helps others. Many young people today abide by the principle, "Service is the purpose of life." However, some people are too bureaucratic in what they do. They like to make things difficult for others and enjoy inconveniencing others. They do not want to accommodate anyone or serve others with a true heart. They not only fail to make good connections with people this way, but they also reveal how incompetent they truly are. Whenever there is a request for help, competent people will generally respond by saying, "OK! OK!" On the other hand, incompetent ones will turn down any appeal for assistance by saying, "No! No!" So we should often reflect a little to see which type of person we are. If we are always saying "no" to others, there must be a problem with our abilities. But if we are always enthusiastic in helping others, we must belong to the competent type that is willing to help others.

2. Be someone who is accommodating but does not follow blindly. All things in the world result from having the right causes and conditions coming together. If we indulge in self-admiration, we will find it difficult to get

support anywhere we go. Therefore, in dealing with others, even if something does not meet our wishes, we should still be accommodating so that we will not be left out. However, being accommodating of circumstances does not mean following blindly. If we are dealing with a malicious person always intent on doing harm, we should not follow his or her example. Therefore, in conducting ourselves, we should accommodate changing conditions without changing our principles. We should cooperate without being partisan, and accommodate others without following blindly.

3. Be someone who emulates the virtuous. Confucius said, "Within a group of three, there is always one who can serve as my teacher." When we hear the wise words others say or about a kind deed they do, we should learn from their example. Even when they act improperly, we can also reflect on their mistakes. This is called "using the wholesome as principle and the unwholesome as warning." We need to know how to learn from others. Sometimes even a young child can have something to teach us. If such a person can be our benevolent teacher, how much more so the virtuous and capable? We should thus be humble in seeking the advice of others and emulating the virtuous.

4. Be someone who is happy and detached from worries. We were not born into this world to bear suffering and worries, so we should not live with a long face every day, dwelling in sorrow, worries, and disappointments. Such a life will offer no joy whatsoever. After a disciple accidentally dropped his prized orchids, Chan Master Jindai explained, "I did not plant orchids for the sake of getting angry." We should therefore all try to create for ourselves an optimistic, progressive, and joyful personality infused with liveliness and laughter. When we learn to live in happiness and distance ourselves from worries,

sorrow, and trouble, life will indeed be more meaningful and valuable.

People are attracted to certain individuals because they are as pleasant as spring breezes, whereas others are so disagreeable that everybody wants to stay as far away as possible from them. What kind of person are you? What kind of person would you like to become? It depends entirely on how you conduct yourself.

The Four Principles of Life

In conducting ourselves, we accommodate circumstances without changing our principles. In other words, we should not merely go with the flow as we also need to adhere to our principles and not alter them in the face of changing circumstances. The following are four principles we should keep:

1. Courtesy is the foundation for handling people and situations. It is the guideline for human relationships and the benchmark for ethical conduct. When we behave courteously, it is easier for us to maintain appropriate and harmonious relationships. Therefore, courtesy is a basic condition in getting along with others, and it must be cultivated from a young age. From our parents and teachers, we learn the proper manners between old and young, senior and junior. Having courtesy, we should always abide by these manners, so as not to err in dealing with people and situations.

2. Righteousness is the prescription for dealing with people. The Chinese character for "righteous" shares the same root with "beauty" and "kindness." As such, the beauty and kindness manifested by the "self" is "righteousness." Confucius said, "Righteousness is the mark of a gentleman." Those who are righteous will only accept material gain when it is right to do so. Moreover, in dealing with people and situations, they will always lend a helping hand, not renege on a promise they have made, and not shy away from the call to duty. Therefore, righteousness is the prescription for dealing with people. Those who lack this quality will have difficulty with friendships. We need to be righteous in order to be noble.

3. Integrity is the way to face the world. People with integrity are upright in character. Officials with integrity know how to care for and love their citizens, and people with integrity have self-respect. In facing the world with integrity, we will not be greedy. Without greed, we will not be enticed by profit or commit any deeds that may harm our character or hurt society and humanity. Therefore, integrity is the way to face the world.

4. A sense of shame is the secret to cultivation. A person with a sense of shame is humble and repentant. A person without a sense of shame is like a tree without bark, while having a sense of shame is like being dressed in beautiful garments. This quality differentiates humans from animals, because without it, a person will commit evil deeds and lose his or her human nature, becoming indistinguishable from animals. So as humans, we need to know shame. We should be ashamed of what we do not know, the skills that we do not have, and all that is impure in ourselves, because a person without a sense of shame can never improve or succeed. Therefore, "knowing shame is as good as having courage." When there is a sense of shame, a person can certainly accomplish great things.

In conducting ourselves, we need to be ordinary as well as extraordinary. By being ordinary, we should be affable and humble. By being extraordinary, we have to be very clear about our ethics, our character, our sense of righteousness, our gains, successes, and failures, as well as what we can and cannot do.

Six Secrets to Getting Along

A swallow cannot fly away from the flock by itself because it will easily get lost. Similarly, people cannot live by themselves away from a community, because they cannot survive well alone. Therefore, people must learn how to get along within a group. The following are six secrets to getting along with others:

1. In listening, understand what we hear. Listening is an art. In listening to others when they speak, we must appreciate what is said. We cannot take meaning out of context or only understand half of what is said. Many people do not know how to listen well. As a result, their biases and misunderstandings of what is said create gossip and rumor. Therefore, in listening, we must pay full attention and listen to all that is spoken. Moreover, by listening carefully, we should analyze and not accept everything without reflection. And in listening to what is said, we must think positively. This is considered "positive listening." Only those who are good listeners can fully appreciate "the sound beyond the musical strings" or "the meaning beyond the words."

2. Our demeanor should be gentle. There's a common saying, "We may know someone's face but not someone's heart." It may be difficult to tell what another person is thinking. However, it is easier to tell from someone's demeanor if he or she is angry, happy, sorrowful, or unhappy. Since our emotions can be communicated to someone else very naturally, in getting along with others, our demeanor must be gentle so that people will enjoy being near us. This is so they can see we are warm, friendly, and easygoing. A person with a gentle

face and happy smile is someone who can make connections easily with others.

3. Be cautious in dealing with situations. In conducting ourselves, we need to "speak with honesty and trust; behave with caution and respect." When we work with others on various projects, we have to think things over carefully and only come to a decision if it is feasible. After agreeing to something, we must fulfill our commitments, and not haggle over details afterwards, for that would be very unwise. As the saying goes, "It is not difficult adjusting to change in the world; the difficulty lies in being cautious." Therefore, before making any decision, we must exercise caution.

4. Ask for advice when in doubt. We are not born with knowledge and have to learn in order to become knowledgeable. When we come across things that we do not know or questions we cannot answer during the learning process, we must be humble and ask for guidance. We can only gain knowledge when, recognizing our limitations, we are brave enough to ask others to teach us. It not only shows our humility, but also our willingness to improve ourselves.

5. Think three times when feeling angry. In dealing with others, it is inevitable that there will be opposing views and conflict. People may want to embarrass and hurt us, and not allow us the means to free ourselves from our plight. When faced with such situations, most people will naturally get angry and their tempers will instantly flare up. However, when we are about to lose control, we need to stop and think for a moment: "Is this worth it?" "Is this excessive?" "Can getting angry resolve any problems?" If we can think three times before we act and be always half a beat ahead of losing our temper, we can naturally put out the flames of anger and not ruin relationships.

6. Only accept appropriate compensation. In working with others, it is normal to share in any resulting gains. However, we should never accept illegal or immoral benefits. According to the *Treatise on the Samadhi of the Precious King* [*Baowang Sanmei Lun*], "In face of gain, we should not fight for a share. In fighting for gain, our delusions and ignorance will be stirred." Therefore, in seeing others make gains, we should not think of getting a piece of the pie or be jealous of what they have. Instead, we should share in their joy and offer our blessings. Thus, our delusions and ignorance will not be stirred.

The secrets to getting along with others in a group are actually not difficult. The difficulty lies in putting them into practice. As long as we have the interests of others in mind and are willing to accept a loss, we will not find it difficult to get along with others.

Standards for Human Relationships

In life, we have to get along with our family, neighbors, friends, and coworkers on a daily basis. When human relationships are going well, our everyday life will be pleasant and our work smooth and fulfilling. Therefore, we need to learn well how to form harmonious human relationships. The following are four standards for consideration:

1. Greet others with sincerity and truthfulness. The most valuable thing in human relationships is sincerity. When we treat others with sincerity and honesty from the bottom of our heart, we will win their trust. Some people are hypocritical and glib in their speech, earning the dislike of others. Worse still, people around them will become defensive and be on their guards. When we immediately put up fences upon first meeting one another, how can human relationships be harmonious? Therefore, on meeting people for the first time, we should give others the impression we are sincere and truthful, then naturally, we will earn their friendship.

2. Treat others with courtesy and respect. People all want to be treated with courtesy and respect. In dealing with our family, neighbors, coworkers, or friends on a daily basis, it is important is to be courteous and respectful. No one will blame us for being too polite. Buddhism even teaches us to "seek the Dharma through respect." If we can treat people with a little more courtesy and respect, we are actually helping ourselves, for later on it will be easier to get things done.

3. Get along with others with a neutral mind in equanimity. In human relationships, there is a saying, "friendship between the wise is as light as water." When friendship

becomes overly intimate, even the best of friends will find it difficult to sustain the relationship. Sometimes because they fail to keep an appropriate distance, conflicts will be inevitable. Therefore, it is best to get along with others with a neutral mind in equanimity, so that friendships will be able to last and grow more fragrant over time.

4. Encourage and support others with knowledge and moral standards. The wise are friends of morality and the crooked with profits. Truly good friends should be each other's benevolent guide and counselor; in other words, "friends should be honest, forgiving, and knowledgeable." Therefore, we should encourage and learn from each another's knowledge and moral standards, because they are the basis for establishing our lives and careers. Given that we all need to work on right understanding, right speech, and right conduct, it is especially important to build friendships based upon moral standards and knowledge, which enables us to motivate each other in these areas.

Dr. Hu Shi, a modern Chinese philosopher and scholar, once said, "What we wish to reap is determined by what we sow." This also applies to standards for human relationships: "We should treat others the way we want them to treat us."

The Way of Dealing with the World

Here is a cat and mouse joke. A cat tried to catch a mouse, and the latter hid in its hole for a long time. The cat started to imitate a dog's bark and the mouse thought: "The cat must be frightened off by the dog." So it came out of its hole without the slightest care and was immediately caught by the cat. The mouse found this hard to accept and asked, "I heard a dog barking just now; how come you are still here?" The cat proudly replied, "At times like these, if you don't speak a second language, how can you possibly think you can survive?"

In our quest for survival, we too will need certain survival skills in hand that will enable us to deal with the world. Here are four suggestions concerning how to deal with the world:

1. Patience is the strength for practice. The most powerful strength in life is patience. It is not about accepting a loss or being incapable, rather, it is about how we resolve our difficulties with an open and clear mind when faced with slander and criticism. In a world of patience, there is no anger or jealousy, but only peace and tolerance. Patience is the ultimate gift in dealing with people and handling situations. Because the earth can bear all trampling and stomping, it can embrace everything and everybody. As such, the all-forbearing earth is also the most ample and solid. Therefore, in conducting ourselves, we must be like the earth, possessing the cultivation to tolerate and embrace, in order to gain the strength to deal with worldly matters.

2. Magnanimity is the cultivation for proper conduct. The universe is immense because of its ability to embrace all phenomena. In conducting ourselves, we must have the capacity to tolerate others before we can gain their

respect. If we are always picking on the faults of others, refusing to forgive or bear with even their smallest mistake, while at the same time demanding others to tolerate us in turn, we are only revealing how petty we are. A glass may only hold ten ounces of water, but a teapot fifty; a 2,000 sq. ft. building may hold three hundred people, but a 10,000 sq. ft. one may hold two thousand. Accordingly, our achievements hinge on how magnanimous our heart is. The larger its capacity, the more it can hold, and the more we can achieve.

3. Gentleness is the prescription for handling matters. In handling matters, we must be moderate and calm, for in so doing we can overcome harshness. Water is most gentle, yet it can go through the hardest rock over time. Therefore, in conducting ourselves, we must handle matters with a gentle heart and calmness; then even the most difficult problem can be smoothly resolved. The secret to self-management is learning to manage our heart first. When we can manage our heart so that it is both compassionate and gentle, no longer differentiating between self and others, then we will have achieved the highest level in self-management.

4. Gratitude is the resource for cherishing our blessings. In conducting ourselves, we must have the virtue of gratitude. People who are grateful cherish what they have, enabling them to go on to repay others in return. As the saying goes, "Repay the generosity of a drop of water with a gushing spring." Gratitude is the wealth of life, and the lives of those who are grateful are the richest.

When we can properly manage our actions, speech, and thoughts without worry, trouble, or conflict with others, we will have gained the best prescription for dealing with people and situations. "Take joy in the practice of gentleness and patience; settle in loving-kindness, compassion, joy, and equanimity." This is the way to deal with worldly matters.

Prescription for Treating Others

How we treat others is a matter of learning as well as an art. For instance, we should act in accordance with what others like and avoid what they dislike. Moreover, we should humbly learn from the strengths of others and be tolerant of their shortcomings. All in all, how we treat others hinges on meeting their needs with skill and consideration, as well as compassion and wisdom. There are the following six points to consider:

1. When people have a strong personality, win them over with gentleness. In dealing with others, if they are strong-minded and we are also firm and upright, the resulting clash of personalities will hurt both parties. Therefore, when the other person is riding high in their power, and taking a tough stand, we should win him or her over with gentleness. When we are yielding and tolerant, we will be able to "overcome toughness with gentleness" and "gain harmony with patience."

2. When people scheme, inspire them with sincerity. Some people like to constantly scheme and plot. In dealing with such people, we should not be like them because when we become deceitful and crafty, it not only drains our energy, but also hurts everyone's feelings. Instead, we should treat them with sincerity because over time, they will certainly be influenced by our candor.

3. When people are angry, subdue them with reason. Some people react to situations impulsively, losing their temper easily. So when they rely on anger, we should use reason to subdue them. As the saying goes, "With reasoning, we can go anywhere." When we have reason on our side, we can win any debate and be able to stand firm.

4. When people are deceitful, treat them with honesty.

Some people often speak without honesty, and act without integrity. In dealing with people who are dishonest in both speech and action, if we also follow suit, we will find it hard to get along. Therefore, even when others are trying to deceive us, we still have to treat them with honesty. "Genuine gold fears not the fire's tempering heat." Therefore, only when we treat others with a true heart will friendships be able to last.

5. When people are malicious, we repay them with kindness. "Those who regularly commit unrighteous acts will inevitably invite their own downfall." We should always have kind thoughts and practice benevolence in order to increase our merits. Some people, however, often treat others with malice instead of goodwill. If we, in turn, treat them the same way, we are only stooping to their level. Therefore, even if others are malicious in their behavior, we still have to show them kindness. Being able to treat people with a kind heart is the greatest benefit we can give to others.

6. When people are volatile, ground them with firmness. Some people are like weather vanes, constantly shifting with the wind and never stable. When others keep changing, we must stay firmly grounded. When we know how to face all changes without changing our stance, we will not lose our focus.

In getting along with people, as long as we treat them with compassion, they will certainly reciprocate with kindness. With more respect and tolerance between people, there will be greater harmony and less conflict in society.

Facing the World without Resentment

The greatest ignorance in life is bitter resentment! When we live in poverty or our talents are overlooked at work, we are often full of complaints about our plight. Sometimes when we lack wisdom and capabilities, we resent the heavens and the people around us. How to face the world without complaint and bitterness is a lesson we must all learn in life. In getting along with others, we need to not only ensure that no one bears any grudges against us, but also not allow ourselves to have too many complaints either. The following four points refer to how to face the world without resentment:

1. Lean on benevolent friends. We should make benevolent friends. The ancients said, "When we learn on our own without any friends around, we will become ignorant." The sutras also teach that, "Benevolent friends are the first ones we should approach." When our body is sick, we consult a doctor, and when our mind and spirit are ill, we need benevolent friends to advise us about our problems. For instance, when we harbor grievances, worries, and complaints in our hearts, close benevolent friends can be our counsel. If all the friends around us are benevolent, they will tolerate us and not bicker and complain about us. Therefore, we should cultivate benevolent friends, and lean on kind people.

2. Don't be jealous of another's success. Where does resentment come from? Most of the time, they are based on jealousy. Because some of us cannot bear seeing others do well, such as when we hear our friends getting a promotion or our neighbors being prosperous and wealthy, we come to feel uncomfortable. We may start out feeling rejection and envy, and eventually we will resent them. Actually, when others are doing well, we

should not only be happy for them, but we can even take a little pride in their glory. When we are not jealous of what others possess or have accomplished, we will not harbor any bitterness.

3. Rejoice in others' accomplishments. Buddhists often vow to liberate all sentient beings. However, when we are unwilling to see others making gains, how is it possible for us to wish for their attainment of Buddhahood? Therefore, in learning and practicing the Dharma, we must first cultivate magnanimity in sharing the joy of others' success. We should rejoice when others gain a good reputation or when they are praised as being learned and ethical. We should celebrate the achievements of others, because when we possess such tolerance and generosity, we will no longer bear any resentment.

4. Appreciate the intention of benevolent words. The Buddha identified "not appreciating words of benevolence" as one of the five traits of "inhumanity." No matter how many good things are said, some people simply fail to appreciate their meaning. Likewise, regardless of how many good deeds you perform, they just cannot see the virtue in them. This is because their minds lack goodness, kindness, and beauty. They are poor at heart because they do not have any nourishment or resources inside themselves. With such spiritual poverty, it is easy to complain. However, when we can appreciate the intention of benevolent words, we will not only be able to hear and embrace kind words, but also see and appreciate good deeds. Then naturally, we will not bear any resentment.

Humble Table, Wise Fare states, "With simplicity, there is no gain or loss; with tolerance, there are no resentment," "In understanding cause and effect, we will not blame the heavens; and in understanding ourselves, we will not complain about others." All in all, we should live in harmony with few complaints.

Life through the Mirror

When we use a mirror, it helps us to see how we look externally. When we use people as a mirror, we can understand our gains and losses. We need to look at ourselves often in the mirror to ensure that we look clean and neat. But in conducting ourselves, we have to use others as examples, because "the benevolent can be our guidance, while the wholesome can serve as a warning." The strengths and weaknesses of others can also serve as our model and a warning. The following are four ways of seeing life through the mirror:

1. Demeaning others is demeaning ourselves. Life is basically a mirror. What we do on a daily basis will be reflected truthfully in the mirror. Therefore, in conducting ourselves, we need self-reflection at all times, in order to see our true self. For instance, if we are arrogant and demean others, we are actually showing how inadequate we are in our cultivation and how shallow we are in wisdom and tolerance. Over time, other people will also look down at us the same way. Therefore, demeaning others marks the beginning of self-humiliation.

2. Respecting others is respecting ourselves. In getting along with others, what is most important is to have respect for one another. When we do not respect others, they will not respect us either. For instance, when others speak, we should listen until they have finished as a way of showing our respect. We need to respect others' views when they are expressed by allowing them to be conveyed fully. Sometimes, we cut people off in the middle of a sentence or start criticizing before they have finished. These are all the habits of disrespect.

3. Being considerate and forgiving of others is being con-

siderate of ourselves. It is often easy for us to blame others for one thing or another. However, when it is our turn to be put on the spot, how good are we? Once, a baseball game had reached a fever pitch, and the spectators were all caught up in the heat of the moment. All of a sudden, someone shouted, "Change the batter! Change the batter!" After a while, another person added, "Change the pitcher! Change the pitcher!" Eventually, somebody even yelled, "Change the umpire! Change the umpire!" Finally, someone said, "Change the spectators! Change the spectators!" Because these people were unable to be considerate of other people, they really did not deserve to watch the game. Therefore, being considerate and forgiving of others is actually being considerate of ourselves.

4. Fulfilling others is fulfilling ourselves. Everything in the world is the result of causes and conditions. Conditions are interdependent; they are the means for us to help each other succeed in what we do. Amidst the endless cycle of causes and conditions, if our thoughts are only for our own interest, our achievements will be limited. When our thoughts are for the benefit of others, we will be able to make broad connections. Therefore, we should never be selfish and only protect our own interests. When we help others, they will help us in return; when we serve them, they will also serve us. Therefore, fulfilling others is fulfilling ourselves.

People are like a mirror for us. Smart people correct their own faults through the mistakes of others. Wise people enrich their experience through the experiences of others. Others are our mirror and our model.

Life's Four "Mosts"

It is the wish of every person to stand head and shoulder above other people and to achieve a few "mosts" in life, such as being considered the most compassionate, the most capable, the most promising, the most successful, or the most intelligent. Since "most" means being "first" or "greatest" in something, it is indeed quite remarkable for someone to achieve a few "mosts" in his or her lifetime. In the *Sutra on the Treasury of Truth*, there are four kinds of "mosts" that should be considered life's four "greatest" goals. They are as follows:

1. Health is the greatest benefit. Although it is the hope of every person to be wealthy, famous, and powerful, these things can never prevent anyone from getting sick. Nothing can ever replace health. Since "every accumulation eventually dissipates and loftiness is the sure sign of failure," health is the greatest wealth we can possibly possess. As long as we are healthy, we have the power to create a better future. Therefore, to be free from sickness is the greatest benefit.

2. Contentment is the greatest wealth. As the saying goes, "while humans die for money, birds die for food." If we are insatiably greedy, no matter how hard we toil through life, we will never escape the suffering from thirst and craving. The Daoist sage Laozi said, "Trouble is nothing more than not knowing contentment." Larceny, theft, corruption, bribery, and embezzlement are always committed by those who cannot find contentment with their present situation. Su Dongpo also said, "Human desire is infinite, but the things that can satisfy our insatiable greed are limited." No matter how much money there is in the world, it is nothing more than what brings food to

the table. It really does not matter how powerful a person is because nobody is exempt from death–the dissolution of the four elements of earth, water, fire, and wind. Therefore, Confucius' disciple, Yan Hui, did not stray from the joy afforded by "a simple dish of rice and a single cup of water." Likewise, the celebrated poet Tao Yuanming found contentment in "leisurely gathering chrysanthemums by the eastern fence." Both examples illustrate that the greatest source of wealth is contentment.

3. Trust is the greatest affiliation. Trust is an expression of respect for others. Confucius said, "Without trust, people have no place to stand." In order for a person to be well-liked, he or she must be credible, dependable, and trustworthy. Similarly, for a government to exercise its authority, it must have the people's trust. According to the *Book of Changes* [*Yi Jing*], "People are assisted by trust." If we are to be trusted, we must be honest since that is the only way for people to truly place their confidence in us, and regard us as their best friends beyond any doubt. For example, it is trust that determines our relationships with our coworkers, employers, clients, family members, and friends. It is being trustworthy that allows us to have meaningful associations and long-lasting friendships. Therefore, trust is our greatest affiliation.

4. Nirvana brings the greatest peace of mind. Everyone hopes for a happy life without worry and heartache. However, worldly pleasure is not eternal, for it is always followed by feelings of loss when it ceases to exist. Hence, pain and suffering are the constant companions behind pleasure. For instance, both worldly and social pleasures are nothing but fleeting moments of physical indulgence. We should, instead, strive for true happiness that is *nirvana*. What then is *nirvana*? It is liberation, the

sense of being carefree that results from the eradication of greed, desire, defilement, and unhappiness. It is the greatest peace of mind.

Each of these four kinds of "mosts" outlined in the *Sutra on the Treasury of Truth* provides us with a useful blueprint for happiness in life.

The Four Necessities of Life

What is most important in life? Because our goals and needs are different, it is difficult to answer this question. Some people think that life itself is most precious, because without life, all fame and fortune are just worthless dust. For others, while life is certainly precious, love is even more valuable. However, there are also people who believe that for the cause of freedom, both can be given up. Generally speaking though–besides the basic necessities of life–joy, contentment, a good reputation, and doing good works are needed by all. Together they constitute the four necessities of life.

1. Joy is the best medicine in life. We all face many problems in life, such as worry, suffering, sorrow, and disappointment. They are the major illnesses in life. When our mind is not healthy, it is difficult for us to progress. So what do we do when we experience sickness in our mind? Joy, openness, optimism, and enthusiasm are the best cures. When we feel there is hope in our future, one that fills us with optimism and enthusiasm for life, then happiness, Chan bliss, and Dharma joy will arise endlessly from our heart. They can cure us of the sicknesses of worry, sadness, and grief.

2. Contentment is the source of wealth. Joy comes from contentment, while worry stems from desire. We do not need to pursue fame and fortune. As long as we are content, we will feel fulfilled in life. Since contentment is the source of wealth, dissatisfaction signifies poverty. Some people may be multimillionaires, but they are not necessarily satisfied. Furthermore, they do not really know how to make use of their wealth. They are rich yet poor. On the other hand, there are people who may be

poor financially, but because they can see the beauty of the world, they are filled with joy and contentment every day. Even though they are not wealthy financially, they still live a rich life. Therefore, when we are content with what we have, we are truly wealthy.

3. Reputation enhances our character. Our reputation is our second life, and we should cherish our good name. In this world, if we have no shame, do not respect our character nor cherish our reputation, we are no different from wild beasts. Therefore, it is said in the *Sutra of the Teachings Bequeathed by the Buddha* [*Fo Yijiao Jing*], "The garment of humility is the most dignified." Humility or a sense of shame is like clothes that we can wear to dignify our body and mind.

4. Doing good deeds is the practitioner's nature. "Poise comes from wisdom and beauty from compassion." A practitioner's character comes from doing good deeds. There are many ways to do good deeds. For instance, we can influence others with compassionate words; greet others with compassionate eyes and demeanor; assist others with compassionate hands; and bless others with a compassionate heart. The key here is using our compassionate heart to constantly help people and do good deeds. This is the true nature of a Buddhist practitioner.

The most important thing in this world is to live a healthy, enriched, and dignified life; one that can bring out our natural disposition.

Life's Maxims

Friends are precious because they guide each other towards goodness and lead one another away from error. "Admonition is the best medicine that cures self and others; good advice is the remedy that benefits one another." We often need the mentoring and guidance of friends. But besides the kind advice and wise words of others, we also need to appreciate the meaning of life through our daily experiences, disciplining and elevating ourselves to a higher level. Though our own appreciation is ultimately the best "maxim" to perfect our life, here are four of life's maxims to consider:

1. Impermanence is life's warning. "Supreme success and fame in one's life are but a dream; unsurpassed nobility and fortune cannot escape the law of impermanence." Impermanence is the reality of life. Birth, old age, sickness, and death are all manifestations of impermanence. Because of impermanence, time will pass, and people and situations will keep on changing. Therefore, we must remind ourselves to be on guard when making use of time, opportunities, and life, for we can never afford to slack off. When we are able to understand the truth of the arising and ceasing of conditions through impermanence, we will certainly act more diligent in life.

2. Dedication brings merit in dealing with matters. When dolphins perform their best, the audience applauds. When we give our best effort in whatever we do, we will have no guilt or regret during self-reflection. In our daily life, we should do our best as long as it benefits and does not harm humanity. In addition to giving our best effort, we also need to do as much good as we possibly can. When we dedicate ourselves fully to what we

should do, we gain merit, and whether or not we actually succeed in our effort will not be the most important thing.

3. Composure provides focus in facing danger. People panic easily when faced with danger. When we become nervous and scared, chaos reigns. Therefore, in facing emergencies, we must first calm ourselves down. By being cool-headed and steady, we will be able to take appropriate action to save ourselves and others. The late philosopher Fang Dongmei almost drowned swimming one time. After he calmed himself down and stopped struggling with his attachment to life, he managed instead to survive the perilous incident. Confucianism teaches, "Be calm so you can focus; when you are focused, you can think clearly; in thinking clearly, you can gain peace." Therefore, use composure to stay focused when facing danger.

4. Compassion is the foundation for practicing charity. Compassion is refined love. It is the selfless contribution without the expectation of a reward. When we give with a compassionate heart, we will have no ulterior motives or greed, but base our intent solely on benefiting humanity. When there is compassion, the world is bright and full of hope. If we treat other living beings with compassion, then even trees, plants, and flowers will naturally repay us with lushness and beautiful blossoms; insects and birds will thank us with melodious chirping and song. Wherever compassion goes, everything will respond positively. Using compassion to benefit people and support all beings is fundamental to being human.

Rivers need the right channel to flow into the ocean. Our lives require maxims to bring us to the right path.

Life Is Like Driving a Car

In order to live safely in this world, our conduct must be lawful and orderly like cars having to observe traffic regulations on the road. In this sense, life is like driving a car. The following are five analogies:

1. To avoid speeding, one must observe proper limits. We all know that speeding can be hazardous, and if we are not vigilant with respect to our own limits in life, it would be as dangerous as exceeding the speed limit on the road. In contrast, if we all abide by our own place and limits, not only will we observe the traffic regulations, but we will also not transgress in our conduct. Each and every car that observes the traffic regulations ensures the smooth flow of traffic and safety on the road. Likewise, when we abide by our proper limits in life, we will be safe in our place and dutiful in shouldering our responsibilities. When we abide by proper limits, we can ensure a happy and safe life.

2. To give pedestrians the right of way, one must be yielding. Some drivers tend to speed through crosswalks, not yielding at all to pedestrians. This behavior shows a lack of respect for the lives of others and ourselves. According to *The Doctrine of the Mean*, "The world is peaceful, for the virtuous are deeply respectful." If everyone can be yielding, there will be no conflicts. During the Period of the Warring States, the prime minister of Zhao was willing to yield the road to the state's most powerful general, who had planned to openly insult him. By yielding, the prime minister not only humbled the arrogant general, but he also achieved the greater goal of enlisting the general's support in preventing the

invasion of the Qin armies. Therefore, yielding can ensure a peaceful life that is stable and harmonious.

3. To stop at railroad crossings, one must have patience in dealing with circumstances. Tragedy is just around the corner for those who are in a mad rush to beat an oncoming train just to save a little time. As the saying goes, "Failure to forbear in small matters spoils great undertakings." A moment of patience may bring longevity to one's life. It can also be the source for accumulating strength. For example, the ruler of Yue had allowed himself to endure humiliation for a time so he could avenge the defeat of his state. As a result, he was able to rise to power again. This illustrates how a life of patience can bring about greater accomplishments.

4. To not run a red light, one must have restraint. Some people will knowingly risk the danger of running a red light. They are like people who willfully disregard the traps of sensual pleasures and deliberately indulge themselves, thereby becoming helpless slaves to materialism. If they persist in their indulgences, they will certainly degenerate morally and spiritually. As the saying goes, "Droplets of water can pierce a stone." If we know how to exercise restraint, and not aggressively seek a foolish and risky lifestyle, we will surely have a safe and happy life.

5. Not to honk unnecessarily, one must be reticent. Good drivers never honk their horns unnecessarily because they can remain calm under any circumstance and navigate their way through traffic by maintaining the right speed and distance. They are like those with virtue, learning, and cultivation in life, who know how to respond to any situation as needed, even be reticent if necessary, and never speak inappropriately. Such people will always think twice before doing or saying anything that would generate gossip or rumor. Therefore, a life of

reticence is a life of cultivation and propriety.

Life is like driving a car. We need to cultivate these qualities in order to ensure a smooth and safe journey.

The Worries of Life

Our future is filled with unpredictable changes. When faced with worries, as long as we are able to step back and think, we can overcome them ourselves. This is the best way to deal with worries. The following are four "worries" to think about in life:

1. Do not worry about having too few children but rather about their ability instead. In agricultural times, every family required a large number of farmhands to till the land. Therefore, people all wished for many children and grandchildren, and thus, the saying, "the more children and grandchildren, the greater the fortune." In reality, even when there are many children, if they are neither well-educated nor brought up with enough love and attention, they will just end up being good for nothing. It is therefore, much better to have fewer children and to teach them well, so they can be strong in both skills and morals. Then, they will bring honor to the family and will not pose a threat to society. So we should not worry about not having enough children but rather, the extent of their ability.

2. Do not worry about how small of an inheritance but rather protecting it instead. According to a Chinese saying, "Fame and fortune will not last more than three generations." That is often the scenario for many wealthy families where the ancestors have worked very hard to establish the family business. They would leave behind a rich legacy for descendants who have not suffered any of their ancestors' difficulties. As they do not appreciate how nothing comes easily, they often squander their inheritance in no time. It is not unusual that the accumulation of wealth over three generations is squandered

in one. So while it is difficult to build a business, maintaining it is even harder. We should, therefore, not worry about leaving too little behind for the next generation; rather we should worry about profligate children not being able to protect their inheritance. Therefore, some people now realize that instead of leaving money and property to their children, it is best to equip their descendants with expertise and skills.

3. Do not worry about a decline in the family's fortune but rather the lack of will and ambition instead. Everything is impermanent in this world, so nothing remains unchanged. It is only natural for fortunes to rise and fall and families to prosper and decline. Some families may face a downturn in their fortune but are saved by capable descendants who make it prosper again. On the other hand, a prosperous family business may only nurture wasteful children who will one day squander it all. Therefore, do not worry about the fluctuations of the family's fortune, worry about your children's lack of the will and ambition to turn misfortune around and bring back honor and wealth instead. This lack will become the true misfortune.

4. Do not worry about not having enough friends but rather falling into the wrong company instead. "Even strict teachers are not as good as benevolent friends." From a young age, we should keep company with good friends and learn the right etiquette in conducting ourselves. Which people are worthy of our friendship? According to the ancients, "Friends that are righteous, forgiving, and knowledgeable." In other words, friends should have a broad knowledge, be righteous, and be forgiving of one another while helping each other to correct their faults. We do not need too many such friends, because as long as we have just one or two, we have something valuable in life. What we should fear is having too many friends

who are deviant, flattering, and harmful, because eventually "one who touches ink will be stained black," for the concern here is that we would be led astray. We should, therefore, not worry about not having enough friends but rather falling into the wrong company, which could ruin our life and our reputation. We must be cautious indeed!

We must be alert to potential crisis in any aspect of our life. We must appreciate the inevitability of living and dying, so as not to become bound by them. Whenever we are able to overcome a worry, there will be one additional ray of light in our life. When we can break through a layer of difficulty, we will come to treasure life even more.

A Happy Life

We seek happiness everywhere, but where is happiness? Is it in money, love, youthfulness, beauty, fame, fortune, status, or power? The truth is that a happy life is where and when we are content, rational, helpful, and benevolent. The following are definitions of a happy life:

1. Be content in life, leaving fortune to our karmic conditions. How do we gain joy and peace in life? Contentment is very important, for if we are not satisfied with what we have, then no matter how much money and property we own, we are only impoverished rich people. On the other hand, if we are content, then even if we only subsist on simple food and coarse tea, we are enriched in spirit. After a meal, the Hakka people in Taiwan will always reply to the question, "Are you full?" with "I'm content." It is important for us to appreciate contentment; otherwise, it will be of no use to us even if we eat gourmet meals every day. When we are content, we are truly happy. Contentment is of prime importance in life because the joy it brings is even better than fame and fortune.

2. Study to gain reason, not fame and fortune. The purpose of learning is to improve our character, become more understanding and reasonable, perform virtuous deeds, and benefit humanity. Therefore in learning, we need to have the right perspective. Some people get an education in order to acquire fame, fortune, or both. If they fail to gain either, they consider their learning worthless. However, through learning, it is more important to gain reason than to acquire fame and fortune.

3. Cultivate morals while helping others without concern

for reward. In life, "having talents is nothing to be proud of; having morals is precious." When we have morals, our mind will not be troubled by gossip or rumor. Therefore, we need morals and ethics in conducting ourselves just as we need high standards for doing things. How then should we cultivate morals? We should refrain from infringing on others, and give them more care and support. We should take simplicity as our teacher. We need to forgive others with the same heart that forgives ourselves. We must repent our mistakes, help others to succeed, and repay any kindness people show us. As a result, our morals will improve and our merits increase over time. In addition, when poor, we are virtuous in not craving; when rich, we are virtuous in giving generously. When we cultivate morals while helping others without expecting any repayment, we can further perfect our ethics and practice.

4. Perform good deeds without calculating gains and losses. Practicing kindness is developing our Buddha Nature, and manifesting the beautiful and kind side of human nature. We need to make broad connections, be happy in practicing kindness, and give willingly. Our life will be broader and our path smoother if we practice benevolence and create positive conditions. Therefore, irrespective of our profession, we need to have the willingness to serve our family, community, society, country, and humanity, giving our best effort in practicing benevolence. As long as what we do benefits the general public, we should not worry about our personal gain or loss. Having the intent to cultivate morals and make connections is the fountainhead of happiness.

The value of life cannot be measured with money. Besides money, there must be other more important meaning and benefit to life. Happiness is certainly one of them.

A Bright Life

A room, which has been dark for one thousand years, will suddenly brighten up with the lighting of an oil lamp. A dark mind will become bright again from repenting and making vows. Brightness is something everyone needs. People admire the sun, the moon, and the stars because they provide the world with light. But we also need to rely on ourselves to create brightness in our life. The following suggestions offer us ways to do so:

1. We need to think correctly. Thoughts are the causes behind reality; reality is the effect of thoughts. Therefore, only with clear thinking can we develop true wisdom. In life, we can have ideals, dreams, or even illusions. We can even think about money, love, a high position, or political office. It does not matter how many ideas we may have. What is important is that we think correctly, otherwise, if the causes are not right, the effects will not be so straight. When our thoughts are not right, our conduct will not be wholesome either.

2. We need to work honestly. Dr. Sun Yat-sen once said, "We need to have the resolve to undertake major endeavors but not necessarily from a position of high office." The truth is, whether we are occupying a political office, taking a job, running a business, or working for wages, we must be honest and concrete in our work. We should not simply put up a front, be devious or perfunctory with our work. A superficial person can never win the recognition of others. Therefore, in conducting ourselves or doing work, we should not depart from being honest and concrete, because only when we approach our work with integrity will our foundation be solid.

3. We need to live joyfully. Seeking a happy life is the

basic goal for everyone. If we live unhappily, what is there for us in life? Therefore, if we are going to live, we should live life joyfully. Life's value and meaning lie in joy, harmony, respect, and peace.

4. We need to learn earnestly. Life itself is endless learning. As children, we learn how to play our role well. Similarly, we should also learn our roles as good parents and conscientious workers. When promoted to a leadership position, we need to learn to perform these roles well too. No matter which stage of life we find ourselves in, it is important to approach our learning with earnest effort and concentration in order for us to perform our roles in life well.

Sunshine, fresh air, and clean water are the three treasures of life. If we can create them within our hearts by having right views, fragrant thinking, wholehearted learning, and pure ideas, we can certainly live a rich and bright life, and our lives would then be filled with brightness and joy.

Harmony through Adapting to Situations

Being able to meet one another in this life means we must have had some connection in the past. It is good if we get along well with each other. However, if we are not interacting well, we should know how to adapt ourselves. Knowing how to adapt ourselves to different situations and achieve harmony can be explained by the following:

1. Be tolerant of people who are sharp and direct. Some people have no consideration for the feelings of others in the way they speak. They will not leave others any room to save face, tending instead to say anything that comes to mind. When they see a small mistake, they will point it out right away. What can we do when we encounter such people? We must be tolerant! Tolerate their ways because direct people are often sharp and we have to bear with them, though we do not have to be as direct and blunt as they are. Instead, if we can treat them with a peaceful, easy, calm, and gentle attitude, then we can naturally reduce their sharpness.

2. Be patient with people who are superficial and unrealistic. Sometimes we meet people who act and speak superficially. They are exaggerated in speech and unrealistic in dealing with matters, for they tend to put up a front with no substance behind anything that they do. We should be patient with their posturing, and not openly correct them or pierce through their facade. As long as we are poised and dignified in our own speech and behavior, and treat people with sincerity, we will be able to check their pretensions.

3. Bear with people who are simple and honest. Some people are so overly honest and straightforward in character

that they are often naïve. When dealing with people who are honest but naïve, we have to bear with their directness. We should not act like we are smarter and mock or laugh at their naiveté. We should, instead, support them so they can bring their honesty into full play, for they certainly have the potential to realize this themselves. In so doing, we can also display our own integrity.

4. Be accommodating of people who are arrogant. Sometimes we come across people who have an arrogant attitude. They like to posture and put on airs. Strutting about like roosters, they appear to be unrivaled in the world. In reality, people like that are not remarkable in any way. They only fear others may look down on them, so they choose to hide behind a mask of pride. We have to accommodate them and not point out their weaknesses. If we criticize their mistakes, it will only harm the relationship. When we accommodate them instead with a humble and yielding mind, and treat them honestly, we will be able to transform them over time. Eventually, they will take down their masks.

Medication is neither precious nor cheap; it is good if it cures. By the same token, a method is neither superior nor inferior; it is wonderful if it works. People are neither fine nor crude; harmony can always be gained when they know how to adapt well to others. No one is absolutely good or bad, wise or foolish. Therefore, we need to learn to accept people's strengths and tolerate their shortcomings. Everyone has talent and potential.

Fortune and Misfortune

Pursuing good fortune and avoiding misfortune is what everyone wishes. However, fortune and misfortune both have their causes and conditions, and the causes of both are the results of human behavior. Therefore, it is said that we create our own fortune and misfortune, the definitions of which are as follows:

1. People who have no self-respect invite humiliation. We must have self-respect. "People must have self-respect before others can respect them; people insult themselves before others insult them." How can we ask for respect when we do not respect ourselves? If we conduct ourselves properly, we naturally will have self-respect, and we will not behave in any way that invites humiliation. Therefore, we must use compassion in dealing with worldly matters and protect ourselves against humiliation with self-respect.

2. People who have no self-discipline attract trouble. We should be lenient with others and strict with ourselves. Self-discipline means we have to manage and discipline ourselves. If we do not know how to discipline ourselves, we will get into serious trouble. For instance, if we indulge in eating, drinking, gambling, and sex, transgress on others in our speech, and break the law with our actions, we may briefly escape the long arm of the law. However, we cannot escape from the Law of Cause and Effect or the admonishment of our conscience. Therefore, for people with an appreciation of cause and effect, they do not need constraints imposed by laws and regulations to exercise self-discipline.

3. People who do not feel self-important gain in benefit. Once an arrogant scholar requested the Dharma from a

Chan master. Without saying a word, the Chan master picked up a teapot and kept pouring into a teacup. The scholar was puzzled and said, "Chan master, the cup is already full." The Chan master replied, "Your mind is like this teacup, already full. Therefore, no matter how good the water of Dharma is, it cannot enter your mind." The scholar was enlightened upon hearing this and became very humble in his attitude. "Arrogance brings harm; humility gains benefit." Being arrogant means setting limits for ourselves. It is like having a poor digestive system, which cannot absorb the nutrients no matter how good the food is. The waste is certainly regrettable.

4. People who are not self-righteous attain broader knowledge. The common mistake we make is to be self-righteous in our views and think little of what others do or say. People who are always self-righteous only succeed in exposing their shallowness. If we are humble, we will be able to learn something new all the time and keep gaining knowledge. Therefore, people who are not self-righteous can gain broader knowledge.

According to the saying, "Fortune and misfortune have no direct access; only people can invite them in." Fortune or misfortune is the result of our own benevolent or unwholesome behavior. "If people practice kindness, though fortune has yet to arrive, misfortune is already far away. If people do not practice benevolence, though misfortune has yet to arrive, fortune is already far away." When we can truly appreciate the causes and effects of benevolent and harmful deeds, we will no longer invite trouble.

Philosophy of Life

We all need to get along with people in our daily life and find ways of working with them. Each person has his or her own way of getting along with others, which becomes part of his or her philosophy of life. The following are suggestions for a "philosophy of life."

1. Not speaking about the faults of others is generous. The worst thing in the world is gossip. While there is no absolute right or wrong in any given matter, the gossip and debate that can ensue from a situation are often quite devastating. Many people are troubled by gossip and can find no peace. They are hurt by gossip and may even lose what they have achieved. Therefore, we become generous when we do not speak about the right and wrong of others. If we encounter others' gossip, it is important that we do not listen to it, do not spread it, and do not come to fear it. When people fail to appreciate the subtleties of human relationships, and are unclear about right and wrong, they will become deluded and emotional. Therefore, we should share directly with people any criticism we may have and not talk about them behind their backs. This way, we will be able to avoid creating any gossip.

2. Not being defensive even when we are right is astute. In getting along with others, it is inevitable that we will be wronged or misunderstood sometimes. Some people will immediately explain and defend their stance in every possible way in order to protect themselves. The truth is that people who are truly wise do not necessarily defend themselves even when they are right. On the other hand, if we have time for self-reflection and are readily able to

admit our mistakes, we are not losing out either, but gaining merit instead. Therefore, we do not have to be so attached to our personal gains and losses, nor is there any need to take to heart every word others say. Slander cannot defeat someone with resolve and ambition, unless that person is lacking in other ways and incapable. The most astute response to slander is not to defend or explain ourselves.

3. Publicizing the kind acts of others is making good connections. Buddhism teaches, "Before attaining Buddhahood, we have to make good connections with people." If we have a heart full of joy, respect, and blessings, then we have the capacity to make good connections with others. It is the best offering for others when we provide them with positive causes and conditions. When we say a few good words on their behalf, and praise them for a kind deed, we are paving the way for them. Making things convenient for others is the best way to create a connection. By being generous in publicizing the kind deeds of others, and regularly praising their virtues, we will also find our own way in life has become smoother, because we have made so many positive connections with people.

4. Not exposing the past mistakes of others is cultivating our virtue. The ancients have said, "Do not hide your conscience; do not publicize the faults of others. Exercise caution in dealing with people, and be without worry. Be patient at work and anything can be settled." In the past, the Chinese accepted it as a virtue to "hide the flaws and publicize the good of others." Nowadays, people are doing the opposite, trying their best to expose the secrets of others. In reality, we need to be empathetic about such matters as we ourselves would not want others to talk about our past either. We should not treat others in a way we do not want them to treat us. Therefore,

people who do not expose the past mistakes of others are virtuous.

There are of course many "philosophies" of life. But if we are able to refrain from "speaking about the right and wrong of others and defending our stance," and further progress to "publicize their virtues while not exposing their secrets," we can certainly make broad connections with people and cultivate more merit. Our journey in life will also be much smoother with fewer setbacks and obstacles to worry about.

Wisdom in Handling Matters

People are either capable or incapable, while situations are neither difficult nor easy. For a capable person, no matter how difficult a situation may be, he and she can handle it very well and bring everything to fruition. However, if a major undertaking is handled by an inept person, it will come off badly with little effect. The most important factor lies in whether wisdom and perseverance are applied when overcoming difficulty. Those who can surmount difficulty are equipped with the wisdom to handle situations as explained below.

1. In taking on difficult responsibilities, we need to apply strength without negative feelings. It is inevitable that we will come across difficulties in what we do. We need the willpower and perseverance to overcome these obstacles, applying extra effort and serious attention required to do the job well. We should never be angry and spiteful or lose our momentum when faced with problems. Moreover, we should not try to suppress those around us with power and authority. Instead, we need to win their trust with sincerity and determination. When we gain the consensus and support of those working with us, any difficulty can be resolved with ease. When we can complete a major responsibility which others cannot undertake, we not only prove our capability, but also enable life to show its full potential.

2. In dealing with difficult people, we need to be aware without speaking. In interacting with others, we need to know how to "tango," when to retreat and when to advance. Often no words even need be spoken. Especially when we are dealing with difficult people, we should "be aware without speaking" as we fully under-

stand what the problems are but do not express them. Because regardless of whether we say anything positive or negative, they will always take every word as a criticism. It is, therefore, best not to say anything at all, but quietly observe their changes. This is the best way to deal with difficult people.

3. In taking a difficult path, we need to be confident and without fear. In learning and practicing the Dharma, we can take either the "difficult path" or the "easy path." Most people consider the practice of reciting the Buddha's name as an easy method that "covers the three levels of practitioners," whereas practicing Chan for enlightenment is the difficult way taken only by practitioners of superior quality. Actually, the most difficult way is the bodhisattva path. Bodhisattvas vow to serve others: "May all sentient beings be relieved of suffering, for I will not seek peace and joy for myself." Because bodhisattvas affirm this vow as the true meaning of their cultivation, they have the confidence to take this path. Thus, they have no fear, are willing to sacrifice themselves, and are capable of accomplishing what is difficult. Therefore, no matter what profession we may be in, we should conduct ourselves like practitioners of the bodhisattva path. In taking this difficult path, we need to be confident and without fear.

4. In enduring suffering, we need to be tolerant without resentment. The sutras say, "The human body is the collection of suffering." Being born as humans, we have to bear the pains of these "eight sufferings": birth, old age, sickness, death, separation from loved ones, encountering our enemies, insatiable cravings, and the ills of the five aggregates of our existence. In addition, we are also afflicted with the various physical and mental sufferings resulting from the discord between self and the environment, external objects, our own mind, and other people.

For instance, we get upset when we hear something disagreeable or see someone behaving inappropriately. In reality, when faced with different situations that are contrary to our views and beliefs, we need to be tolerant and resourceful. We should not become resentful, because the more we complain and hate, the more we add to our suffering. Therefore, in enduring suffering, we need to be tolerant without resentment.

Life afflicted with suffering is like a sharpener. More suffering results in more perseverance, and more afflictions bring more strength.

The Key to Dealing with Tasks

Through work, we test our perseverance, realize our courage and capacity, and prove our cultivation. Therefore, our attitude in dealing with tasks is the key factor to consider in life.

1. Do not be careless because a task is easy. As the saying goes, "Do not take lightly something that seems easy to attain." Very often, because tasks are going smoothly for us, we take them as being too easy and become negligent. Thus, a small job may end in a major disaster. A serious train accident took place in Taiwan because a brake was not applied in time. A crucial mechanism like this seems easy to operate, but a momentary act of negligence left many families forever separated from their loved ones. Therefore, regardless of how small a task is, we should always be cautious, doing it mindfully to avoid any future regret.

2. Do not retreat because a task is difficult. Most people retreat when they encounter obstacles in their work. In reality, success or failure often hinges on whether we can persist through the last five minutes. Therefore, we should have the spirit and courage to take risks that are necessary to overcome difficulties. The more difficult and challenging a task is, the more it can develop our potential, and the more crucial it is that someone is able to undertake it. Therefore, we should not be concerned whether something is easy or difficult. As long as it is beneficial to people, we should bravely overcome the hardship. If we have no fear of setbacks and keep working at it time and time again, we will certainly accomplish the task.

3. Do not slack off because a task takes time. When young

people make a resolution, it is often easy to take the initiative but difficult to follow through. Therefore, when something takes months, years or even longer to realize any effect, some people will become impatient and give up halfway, and thus waste all their previous effort. In reality, an immediate effect is not always apparent in most situations. Scholars in the past had to be able to withstand at least a decade of hard work in their studies before they got the opportunity to succeed. Likewise, when Chinese people in the old days pickled vegetables and sealed them in jars, the longer the containers remained sealed, the better the flavor and aroma. Therefore, young people nowadays should not look for instant results in establishing their career and gaining success in work. They must be patient and persevere over a long time without ever slacking off, before they can be forged into steel.

4. Do not get angry because a task presents problems. When we work with people, it is inevitable that there are differences of opinion. We should not get angry because their views and working styles are not the same as ours and so decide to go separate ways. If our parents and teachers provide us with advice and guidance, we should accept them with humility. We should not consider their suggestions as interference or blame and get upset with them. Furthermore, we should never shirk our duty or ignore our work because of it. Otherwise, we will end up accomplishing nothing. Therefore, we should not get angry because of problems with our work. It is a major mistake we should avoid in dealing with all matters.

There are actually many principles in dealing with tasks. However, if we can apply the above points, we can at least make more progress.

Flaws in Dealing with Others

How well-rounded we are in conducting ourselves can be demonstrated by how we operate. While we need skillful means, we must also abide by our principles, being resourceful while not being devious. For instance, in dealing with superiors or employers, some people resort to flattery and cater to whatever their bosses fancy, with little or no regard for what is right or wrong, good or bad. They ignore the consequences of their actions. This is a practice we must avoid in conducting ourselves. We must be aware of the following explanations regarding the problems of dealing with others.

1. Pleasing others to suit their fancy is deceit. In conducting ourselves, we can never deceive heaven above, people below, our inner conscience, or the outer world. Transgressing on others does not necessarily just include violating others through force or hiding the truth with lies. Some people also have no regard for whether another is right or wrong, good or bad in what they do. They only cater to their likes and dislikes with the intention of winning special attention so that they may profit from it. Such behavior is deceiving both self and others, which only undermines our character and brings harm to others.

2. Flattering others is pretense. Some people are good at flattery, especially with those they intend to please. They will praise the subjects of their flattery in everything they do, even when they conduct unwholesome deeds. People like these are pretentious. They do not differentiate right from wrong in their flattery, even though those around them can tell right away how dishonest they are. In the end, they often cause harm before

they can gain any benefit.

3. Cheating and lying are fraudulent behaviors. "In detecting their fraud, we do not show them we know; in noticing their deceit, the secret lies in not speaking about it." Some people have ulterior motives in befriending others. If their intention is to cheat and profit by it, they will then think of various schemes to achieve their goal. However, even if their friends are taken in by their fraudulent acts for the moment, how long can they really hide their deceitful ways? Furthermore, by the time they are through cheating all of their friends, who would be left for them to take advantage of? Therefore, to cheat and lie can only lead to harm.

4. Honeyed words are lies. According to the saying, "Gourmet dishes cannot do without salt, but honeyed words are not worth a penny." No matter how articulate or well-spoken people are, when their words are without substance, they are still lying. There are people who are good at talking. Their words are as sweet as honey and are always exaggerated. While others may be deluded for the time being, because they do not know the whole story, honesty is always the best policy, and fancy words are never as good as straight talk. Moreover, "our eyes cannot see themselves, our nose cannot smell itself, our tongue cannot taste itself, and our hands cannot hold themselves, but only our ears can hear our own sound." Therefore, we should be cautious in speech so as to cultivate our moral character.

In conducting ourselves, we project our image. Our image is based on the views and feelings others accumulate over time as they see us handle matters and get along with people. Since we reap what we sow, if we want to gain a good image, we must be cautious in conducting ourselves.

The Four Difficulties in Life

A philosopher once said, "The universe is only five-feet high. People six-feet tall need to bow their heads in order to survive within it." This means we inevitably encounter obstacles in life that are difficult to overcome as we try to stand tall and realize our indomitable spirit. The following points explain these "four difficulties in life."

1. It is difficult to be without remorse and guilt in establishing ourselves in life. What distinguishes the morals of the sage from that of a petty individual is that the sage is "without shame in facing heaven above and without deceit in dealing with people on earth below." Moreover, according to the saying, "The wise and holy are always satisfied and composed. The crooked are always worried and uneasy." However, is it possible for most people to be truly free of all remorse and guilt in what they do? For instance, they may question whether they have fulfilled their duty to their country and society, truly honored their parents and seniors; shouldered all responsibilities for their family and dependents; or acted with righteousness and care towards their friends and relatives; and finally, treated strangers and all things within the universe with compassion. If they are totally free of all remorse and guilt in the above obligations, only then would they be close to having a clear conscience in dealing with others.

2. It is difficult to conduct ourselves without ruining our character. A piece of emerald without any defect is a thing of great value. People without any blemish in character are worthy of the respect of others. Therefore, in conducting ourselves we have to maintain our integrity.

However, in conducting ourselves or in getting along with people, is it possible for us to be completely free of faults and defect? For instance, holding public office takes deep cultivation and a strong willpower to be honest in face of bribery, to refrain from being greedy over profit, and to not compromise one's principles when there are setbacks. Society today is like a huge pot of dye, for it is not easy to remain untainted while inside. How many people can truly be like the lotus flower that remains pure as it grows out of the mud? Therefore, it is difficult to remain without any fault in conducting ourselves in life.

3. It is difficult to maintain ourselves without any wrongdoing. In the past, Confucian scholars often said, "When we are intelligent and reasonable, we can make the whole world virtuous. If we cannot, we can at least attend to our own virtues." Many people are good at living according to good moral standards, not breaking the law, or going against public opinion. However, according to the Buddhist teachings, every thought that arises within sentient beings is nothing but unwholesome karma and wrongdoing. With so many intangible thoughts arising, how can we maintain ourselves in life by sustaining purity in every thought without having any unwholesome action or wrongdoing?

4. It is difficult to settle our mind and be without worries and troubles. In life, we all need to find equanimity. There are people pursuing fame, status, money, love, or a successful career. However, no matter where we want to place our focus, there is no guarantee we will be free of worry. Wherever we go, there will be gains, losses, good, and bad. Once our mind centers on pursuing gains and avoiding losses, we will be troubled when we fail to realize our ideals and not find contentment. Therefore, it is difficult to settle ourselves and live without worry.

It is not easy to pursue perfection. Therefore, it is very important for us to put forward our best effort and rid ourselves of remorse, flaws, wrongdoing, and worry as we confront the many difficult circumstances in life.

Matters of Propriety

There is no absolute right or wrong, good or bad in the world. Wisdom lies in having a proper sense of propriety in dealing with all matters in life. For instance, while praising others is a virtue, inappropriate praise becomes insincere flattery, and others will look down on us for doing it. Giving is an act of kindness, but if we publicize what we do widely by using the suffering of others to show off our own kindness, we will attract criticism. The following are four definitions of propriety in how we conduct ourselves:

1. Praising others wins friendship. Words of praise are like the fragrance of flowers. They are pleasant and refreshing. People who offer sincere words of praise to others will certainly gain friends. Therefore, in getting along with people, it is indeed most important for us to know how to praise them. Christians sing hymns of praise to God, and Buddhists often chant the "Incense Praise." Both customs signify that even the Buddha and God need to be praised, not to speak of ordinary people, who need the praise and admiration of others even more so. This is especially the case when someone feels dejected. A few words of praise can turn his or her life around, so that he or she will be able to see hope again. So if we want to gain friendships, praising others with sincerity will certainly help.

2. Flattering others will gain contempt. We should do a good deed every day. This is not difficult to do so because praising others is already a good deed. However, praise is not the same as flattery, because the latter is superficial. According to the saying, "People who like to flatter give rise to gossip." Therefore, we

should rather befriend people who counsel and admonish us instead of those who flatter us. By the same token, we need not fear the criticism of others but rather be afraid of their flattery. When people praise improperly, it will be taken as flattery, which only serves to gain the contempt of others. We should not only refrain from flattery but we should also avoid any inappropriate praise.

3. Sharing joy multiplies happiness. Some people can share success but not suffering, while others may be able to endure difficulties together, but not good fortune. True friends are those who can go through thick and thin together. When we are happy, we should spread it around. Moreover, when our friends achieve fame and fortune, or accomplish some success, we should offer them our blessings with heartfelt sincerity, while sharing in their glory. We must never be jealous or attempt to obstruct them in their endeavors. Life is so beautiful when we know how to share joy with others.

4. Being able to "give without any attachment to form" is true kindness. The ancients recognized the virtue of not letting others know their practice of kindness. In reality, we don't always need to be afraid of demonstrating kindness. Our society needs many kind and beautiful acts to motivate people and encourage benevolence as a social trend. Therefore, those who are sincere in their practice of giving need not deliberately conceal their good deeds. What we do not need are people acting with deceit for the purpose of gaining a good name. They may make a donation to a charitable organization and publicize it widely with the expectation of an immediate reward or praise. Moreover, they may even speak improperly and hurt the self-respect of those receiving their donation. Such antics will only result in losing any kind intent to their giving. Buddhism teaches "emptiness in the three aspects of giving" which means we should not be

attached to the receiver, the gift, or ourselves as a giver. Therefore, any reward we may reap from our generosity should be considered intangible. This would indeed be true kindness.

Each person has his or her own characteristics and style in dealing with people and matters. Above all, we must have integrity and leave space for others. In this way there will be enough room for all to turn around when necessary.

Fundamentals

Trees have roots and water has springs. If the roots are wide and deep, then trees can grow tall and strong. From a spring, water can flow far and long. In conducting ourselves, we also need to pay attention to our "fundamentals" in order to establish ourselves in life. The fundamentals of life are as follows:

1. Knowing propriety and justice is fundamental to conducting ourselves. We have to focus on propriety and justice in life as they are basic to being human. They are what make humans different from animals, such as pigs and cattle. Besides seeking food several times a day, these animals have no other aspirations. However, as a higher order of living beings, humans have to tend to their spiritual and mental lives in addition to clothing, food, shelter, and transportation. People need to build a community with order, ethics, conscience, and justice. Once propriety and justice are lost, we are hardly human anymore and cannot create a human society.

2. Appreciating the big picture is fundamental in dealing with the world and conducting ourselves. This means we must be considerate of others, our community, and our country, because they are the larger part of us. If we only think of ourselves and look after our own narrow interests, ignoring the benefits of society and country, we will not be able to appreciate the big picture in life. We must be mindful of the needs of the community we live in before we can find our niche in society. Therefore, appreciating the big picture is fundamental in dealing with the world around us.

3. Abiding by the law is fundamental to gaining freedom. In getting along with others, people need rules and regulations for everyone to follow so that they will not

infringe upon each other. For instance, the laws of a country, the by-laws of an organization, and the regulations of a school all function as guidelines and boundaries for their members. With guidelines provided by a legal system, no one will transgress the boundaries, and society can function in an orderly manner. In this way, personal freedom will be protected. In Buddhism, the Five Precepts of refraining from killing, stealing, lying, sexual misconduct, and taking intoxicants prevent people from infringing upon the life, property, reputation, trust, and wisdom of one another. Therefore, the Five Precepts are fundamental to being human and getting along with others. If we are unable to uphold the Five Precepts, we are lacking in humanity. To observe them is to abide by the law. This is fundamental to our conduct.

4. Distinguishing right from wrong is fundamental to understanding the mind. There are so many questions of right or wrong, good or bad, in this world that it is very difficult to differentiate between these extremes using absolute standards. Therefore, we cannot rely just on our own understanding to judge others and make demands upon them. However, not having an absolute standard does not mean we should not know right from wrong. In our conscience, we still need to have our own basic standard for right and wrong, good and bad. We must know and understand them clearly so we can have good discernment. With sound discernment free of delusion, we can judge right from wrong, and distinguish good from bad. When we have a clear mind, we will not suffer from any delusions.

   The Great Learning says, "Things have their roots and their branches. Affairs have their end and their beginning. To know what is first and what is last will bring one closer to the Way." When we understand the fundamentals of life, we are close to following the Way.

Things to Avoid in Life

If we want to achieve something in life, we should deal with major undertakings with initiative, resolve, and practice. If we can get rid of all notions of right and wrong between self and others, then everything around us will become our supporting causes and conditions in whatever we do. We should avoid, however, four things in order to achieve harmony in human relationships:

1. We should not be too harsh in criticizing mistakes others make. Nobody is perfect in this world, and no one is exempt from making mistakes. When others err, have shortcomings or bad habits, we should correct them and offer advice. However, we should not attack or criticize them harshly. If we are too severe in our criticism, it is like beating a vicious dog. It will only make it more vicious. Therefore, "we should not be too severe in our criticism of others; we should be considerate of how much they can tolerate." Leaving room for others in any matter is a virtue we should have in life.

2. We should not be too demanding in teaching others. Humanity has been able to progress over time, because there have been people with the capacity to teach, and thus experiences can be passed down to subsequent generations. However, there are overly enthusiastic people who want to show others all that they know. For instance, they may teach others music, painting, or how to use computers, all the while demanding that their students be ethical, compassionate, and skillful in dealing with people and matters. Teaching others is a wonderful thing. However, "in teaching others benevolence, we should not be too demanding, but should ensure they can

cope and follow appropriately." When the standards we set are too high, the student will have trouble keeping up. He or she may find it too difficult or even become turned off by the demands and give up altogether. Therefore, while we should provide guidance untiringly, we need to do so according to the abilities and personality of the student. Such is the right way to teach.

3. We should not be superficial in praising others. While it is a virtue to praise others, we need to do so appropriately. We should not exaggerate or be superficial. Otherwise, people may think that we are being sarcastic. Not only will this incur the opposite effect, but people may also think that we are flattering them to curry favor. For instance, we should praise someone who is compassionate for having compassion, but we do not necessarily have to say that he or she is wise as well. With people who look ordinary, we can say that they have poise, but there is no need to compliment them for being beautiful. Therefore, in praising others, we should do so appropriately and with sincerity. We must never be superficial.

4. We should not be arbitrary in blaming others. Right or wrong, good or bad in this world are not absolute. Sometimes owing to differences in perception, the viewpoint and interpretation of any matter will naturally vary. Therefore, when we blame others for being wrong, we must never jump to conclusions. We should look at the matter from another angle, consider their point of view, and think again for ourselves before we arrive at a conclusion. Someone who can lift a thousand pounds cannot lift himself or herself. This is the best illustration of being clear before blaming others and being critical of ourselves even when uncertain.

"It is easy to see the mistakes of others and difficult to

understand our own shortcomings; it is easy to blame others for their faults and difficult to reflect on our wrongdoing." In getting along with others naturally, we should not contradict feelings or reasoning. When we do not indulge in stirring conflicts between self and others, there will be no gossip. We need to be mindful of the above four things to be avoided in life.

The Four Don'ts in Conducting Ourselves

In conducting ourselves, we have to be kind to others, act benevolently, practice generosity, and make good and broad connections with others. We should do our best in performing any positive, kind, and beautiful act that benefits people. On the other hand, we should reject absolutely anything that may harm others while only benefiting ourselves. This advice is fundamental to how we should conduct ourselves in regard to our morals and conscience. The following are four things we should not do in life.

1. Do not attempt to profit from another's misfortune. There are two sides to human nature, the good side and the bad side. They are easiest to see in times of tragedy and natural disaster. Some people ignore their own safety to rescue the victims of catastrophes, while others may just fold their arms and watch from the sidelines with an uncaring attitude for they think it has nothing to do with them. Worse still, some people not only just stand and watch, but also exploit the opportunity to profit at the expense of another's suffering. Imagine when others are in trouble, we covet their property. When others face misfortune, we add to their trouble. When others fall down, we step on them. Such behavior is truly deplorable! Therefore, we must never take advantage of another's misfortune.

2. Do not make another's problem worse. According to the saying, "In providing relief, we should help people when they lack resources in a crisis." If someone is thirsty, supplying him or her with a glass of water is better than offering a glass of fresh juice at ordinary times. Although there are people in society these days who are willing to provide help in times of difficulty, there are

also many who are ready to make life worse for those in trouble. For instance in Taiwan, there are many physically challenged people trying to scrape a living together as vendors of lotto tickets and other small necessities, but they become the targets of extortion and deceit by thugs. They often lose their small investment and are unable to make ends meet. Their already difficult plight is made much worse by the greed of others. While it is good for us to be able to help others in times of difficulty, if we cannot, the least we can do is not make things worse.

3. Do not stop trying because of a little adversity. The chance of our success or failure in what we do is often fifty-fifty. It all hinges on our wisdom and perseverance in overcoming setbacks. Some people will stop and give up once they encounter a little problem. It is like refusing to eat for fear of choking or infants first learning to walk. If infants stop trying after falling down, they will forever be crawling on the floor. Therefore, when faced with difficulties in what we do, we should look for the core of the problem and find a solution for it. We cannot simply refuse to eat for fear of choking, otherwise, we will starve to death.

4. Do not ignore advice because of personal biases. In their capacity to lead, leaders need to "listen broadly and widely," and "observe and accept advice." They should be open-minded in order to gather good counsel. However, some people just listen selectively. They will only accept the advice of experts, professionals, their superiors or close aides, but not a word from their subordinates or anyone they consider "unimportant." While the words of people in low positions might carry less weight, they are not necessarily useless, because even "the foolish will have something to contribute after a thousand attempts." Therefore, in listening, we should focus on whether what

is said is constructive and inspiring. We cannot afford to ignore advice because of our personal biases towards people, because we may later regret missing these words of wisdom.

In conducting ourselves, we need to have integrity and not take advantage of another's suffering. We also need wisdom, for we cannot be unclear in our reasoning over matters.

Four Things to Guard Against

In dealing with people and situations, we need to appreciate reasoning, reality, people, and human relationships. In conducting ourselves in life, we have to know ourselves and exercise self-discipline, and then progress further by knowing what to guard against. When we are strict in self-discipline and ethics, we have the keys to establishing ourselves. The following are four things we need to guard against in life.

1. Guard against arrogance as it is the worst of all evils. Arrogance is the chief cause of all wrongdoing. Some people speak with disdain and have a superior attitude towards others, which results in others resenting them. Consequently, longtime friends may eventually leave them because of their arrogance, and for the same reason, others would not want to work with them even for a good cause. Therefore, we should not be too proud of our wealth or our talents. We need to appreciate that the more wheat ripens, the lower their stalks bend. So a truly great person is always very humble, because with a broad and open mind, her or she can embrace everything.

2. Guard against being deceitful as it is the thief of all virtue. The Chinese character "trust" consists of the two characters: human and speech. If a person's words are not trustworthy, he or she is unworthy of being human. Honesty is the basic cultivation in conducting ourselves. Some people are hypocritical and deceitful. They like to play little tricks and take advantage of others in small ways. Oblivious to reality, they indulge in their antics thinking nobody else notices. The truth is that others may not want to raise the issue with them at first, but if they keep up with their tricks, they will end up ruining

their own reputation. Eventually, they may become isolated because no one will want to deal with them. In human relationships, it is difficult for us to know a person's heart, so we can only rely on "trust" in getting along with one another. By being deceitful, we are only hurting our relationships with others. Furthermore, losing both our fortune and honor because of deceit, is truly a great loss. Therefore, we must not cheat when dealing with people and situations.

3. Guard against flattering others as it is despicable conduct. While we should be humble in conducting ourselves, we must still have dignity. Being dignified means having virtue and not pursuing power and influence by flattering others for our own gain. People who like to flatter are looked down upon by the wise and righteous. Therefore, those who are wise will not use flattery to delude others and will not be moved by it either.

4. Guard against pretentiousness for it lacks substance. *The Analects of Confucius* [*Lun Yu*]says, "The wise have no dignity if they are superficial." People who are pretentious and superficial in their behavior and speech will find it hard to earn the respect of others. Great personalities like Master Xuanzang "spoke not of fame or fortune; they behaved without any pretension," and Master Zhenguan "would not act in a frivolous manner." Their poise and demeanor are still admired by people today. According to a saying, "People insult themselves before others insult them; people belittle themselves before others belittle them." Therefore, in establishing ourselves, while we should not be arrogant, we cannot be superficial either.

In conducting ourselves and handling matters, we need not worry about others not respecting us, but rather, worry that we do not respect others. As long as we can act with virtue and dignity, cultivating our moral and ethical behavior, we will naturally win the respect of others.

Leadership

In a family, the parents are the ones leading the children. In a state, the governor is the leader. In a company, the business owner leads his or her employees, and in a government cabinet, the secretary in charge is the leader. Leadership is important in stabilizing a country. There is a Chinese saying, "One would rather be the head of a chicken than the behind of a cow." This means that people do not naturally want to be followers. They prefer to lead others. But to be an effective leader, we not only need to have the proper disposition, but we must also know how to lead. The following are keys to leadership.

1. Leaders must be able to act as well as talk. "If someone above is doing well, those below will have a good example to follow." In a leadership position, we must be able to do what we say. If leaders only make demands of their subordinates while acting contrary to their own words, then people below will not accept them. Moreover, if leaders lack morals in their behavior, their followers will act in a similar manner just to please them. Therefore, leaders must lead others with good ethics and set an example with proper behavior. Confucius once said, "If you are upright, others will follow without being ordered to; if you are not upright, they will not follow even when ordered to do so." Therefore, leaders must set a good example for subordinates, and reliably do as they say. As such, even without specific orders being given, subordinates will work hard in their positions.

2. Leaders must not complain or have regrets. Leaders must have a farsighted and optimistic mind. In addition, they need the capacity and perseverance to face difficulties and not regret having given their all to accomplish a task. Dr. Sun Yat-sen, the founder of the Republic of China, once said, "Danger and difficulties are not what

we should worry about. We should have no fear of power and dominance." Therefore, a leader should not fear hard work, but be willing to contribute, like the silkworm giving up all of its silk. Moreover, leaders should be serious and responsible about work without complaining or blaming anyone for their problems. As a result, those below will certainly work with one heart in following their leadership.

3. Leaders must have both compassion and wisdom. Being a leader means assuming the work assigned to us. In addition, he or she must have the ability to assess the need for changes and the wisdom to devise strategies and handle a crisis. Furthermore, a leader must have compassion to help his or her followers in resolving their problems. Leaders should treat whatever happens to their subordinates as their own business, so that the latter will be able to settle down in their jobs with peace of mind and remain loyal. Therefore, leaders need both compassion and wisdom.

4. Leaders must not be selfish or arrogant. A leader cannot harbor selfish motives. A leader cannot unfairly reward or penalize subordinates as he or she pleases. More importantly, leaders should never gain personal profit from public causes or use public resources for private matters. They should understand right from wrong, and be aware of honor and denigration. In addition, they must be fair, humble, and courageous enough to be accountable for any matter. As such, they will win the respect of their subordinates, and everyone will follow the direction of their leadership wholeheartedly.

Two kinds of people are required for any organization to flourish: able leaders and loyal followers. People who are incapable and refuse to accept the leadership of others are the stumbling blocks of the organization. Therefore, we should be happy to be led and also know the way of leadership.

Leading People

As part of society's workforce, we either lead or are led by others. Regardless of whether we lead or follow, we all need to have certain talents and capabilities. But being in a position of leadership, we especially need to possess a strong capacity for thinking, working, handling situations, and personal cultivation, in order to be qualified to lead others. Leading others is a serious art, and the following are guidelines for how we should handle this major responsibility.

1. We need to be well-acquainted with our personnel in order to give proper assignments. The first key to leading people is to know how to make use of their talents appropriately, and then assign them the right tasks. In knowing their strengths and weaknesses, as well as their interests and hobbies, we will be able to bring their talents into full play. We can also better cultivate interest in their work, so that they feel more committed to what they are doing. Furthermore, we should also understand their family background, know their needs and difficulties, in order to provide them with the right assistance and encouragement. This way, they will be grateful for our concern, and will be more likely to settle down in their job and give their best effort.

2. We need to train and educate our personnel in order to assure continuity. In order for an organization to operate on a long-term basis, training is an absolute necessity. Therefore, many corporations and organizations these days provide training for their employees. They allow their workers to go abroad for further education and other training opportunities. Many CEOs and presidents of large corporations, and even leaders of a country, active-

ly train successors for their positions. When we know how to train people, our organization will be assured of good future leadership long after we are gone.

3. We need to rely on our personnel in order to have supportive conditions. A tree cannot replace a forest. No matter how capable a person is, there are still limits. We need to gather the strengths of many people in order to gain collective wisdom and creativity. Therefore, wise leaders always delegate their power to their subordinates by giving them room to test their skills. Moreover, we should have the wisdom and capacity to trust our employees, because "if we employ people, we should not doubt them; if we doubt people, we should not employ them." When we can delegate full authority to them, our subordinates will feel they are trusted. They will then do their best in their work. Therefore, when we make good use of people, we will gain supportive conditions.

4. We need to retain our personnel in order to have room to maneuver. Sometimes our subordinates may want to leave their position, and as supervisors, we must find out the reason. Is there a problem in getting along with coworkers? Is the salary too low? Is the job sufficiently fulfilling for their skills? We need to resolve these problems accordingly and try our best to retain those who are thinking of leaving, letting them feel they will have a good future by staying and that there is hope for advancement. While sometimes we may not be able to retain them, they will still appreciate our intention and realize how much we cherish them. According to the saying, "Human sentiments remain even if no deal materializes." In the future, one of them may become an unexpected supporting condition. Therefore, in trying to retain personnel we leave ourselves room to maneuver.

There are two types of people that help an organization

operate: leaders and followers. If one's ability and strengths are like a sharp knife, such a leader can easily hurt others. On the other hand, with people who can get along with a group, their knives may be a little blunt, but they last longer and will not harm others. Therefore, as leaders, we need to be broadminded and have a spirit of equality. In addition, we must know our employees, train them, use their abilities well, and retain them. In knowing people, we can share the same goals; in training people, we must know how to teach them; in working with people, we must be fair and reasonable; and in retaining people, we must provide them with a future.

Assessing Others

　　We all know what a person looks like physically with a head, four limbs, a height of several feet, and a shape that is either slim or round.　However, people also have their internal world encompassing their thinking, views, ideals, and feelings.　If we could discern their endless thoughts and know whether or not they are kindhearted, we would then be able to truly understand them. How do we understand people?　The following are four keys that can help us:

1. People who are powerful but do not abuse their power are wise.　Some people are endowed with immense power and may think they are unrivaled in the world. They become so authoritarian and arrogant that they just do whatever pleases them with no regard for anyone or anything.　These people are typical tyrants.　On the other hand, others may enjoy much power, but they are not dictatorial.　They do not abuse their power by conducting matters according to their likes and dislikes.　People like these are certainly wiser.

2. People who are rich but not miserly are benevolent. Some very wealthy people are extremely stingy with their money.　As the saying goes, some of them may feel "even if I can benefit the whole world by plucking out a single hair, I will not do it."　Conversely, there are rich people who are very generous and enjoy giving away what they have.　They are indeed compassionate and kind practitioners with an appreciation of the true path.

3. People who are talented but not arrogant are good teachers.　Some people may be very talented, but they are very arrogant because of their expertise.　They look down on everyone around them.　They lack morals and do not

qualify as teachers. People should not allow their talents to breed arrogance. Even though they may be talented, knowledgeable, and learned, they should remain gentle and humble in treating others and dealing with matters. As such, they are equipped with both knowledge and virtue and become worthy teachers and models for others.

4. People who are satisfied but not carried away with success are respectable. Some people get carried away when they are doing well. As a result, they only earn the disdain of others. For instance, when people who have nothing win the lottery, they immediately forget how frugal their life had been. They buy new cars and big houses, eagerly flaunting their new possessions. There are also people who only have very little means, but once they get connected with power and money, they forget about their poor old friends. Such people are vain and unreliable. Even though they may gain momentary glory, it will not last. Others also will not respect them or count on them for anything. Therefore, when we are doing well, we should conduct ourselves as we always have. Buddhism teaches us to have a balanced mind. Whether we are rich or poor, learned or ignorant, having a balanced mind is very precious.

"We can learn the sounds of the birds when we go into the mountains; we can discern the nature of fish when we are close to the water." We can, therefore, easily assess people's character by how they confront poverty, success, honor, humility, prosperity, failure, slander, or praise.

How to View People

We encounter many types of people every day. In the course of interacting with others, we often differentiate between who is good or bad and whom we like or dislike. Observing people is a form of art, as well as a kind of wisdom. Some people only look at others on a superficial level. They may admire someone beautiful or like another who is handsome. There are people who only judge others in passing, admiring their good manners or enjoying what they say. In reality, observing people well involves not just seeing what is on the surface or in the moment. The following are some pointers for consideration.

1. Do not view others as lowly because of their menial jobs. Work is neither superior nor inferior. It is always sacred in any form. We cannot assess someone's character based on the nature of his or her work. Instead, we should follow the wisdom in the saying "Having no status is not inferior, having no shame is." Therefore, we cannot categorize work such as collecting garbage, driving a cab, or being a street vendor as being lowly. In reality, service work is highly valuable. As long as people make money through honest and hard work, every profession can have its own elite core, and every branch of work its own bodhisattvas. Therefore, we can never judge the character of others by the kind of work they do.

2. Do not view others as old because of their age. Life is not just about our physical body. It is about the nature of our mind. Being old has little to do with one's age, but has more to do with one's state of mind. Some people may be old in age, but their spirit and mental energy are flourishing. Their passion in serving society and their resolve in helping humanity cannot even be matched

even by younger people. Therefore, we should not assess someone as old simply by his or her age.

3. Do not view others as impoverished because of their material poverty. True wealth is joy and not material riches. True poverty is ignorance and not the lack of money. Therefore, we cannot evaluate a person's wealth by the amount of money and property he or she possesses. Some people are materially poor, but their will and ambition are not. Compared to most rich people, they are actually superior in character, are more principled, and uphold higher moral standards. As such, they are richer in spirit. Therefore, we cannot consider someone impoverished due to his or her lack of material wealth.

4. Do not view others as insignificant because of their small achievements. The scale of a person's achievement should not be judged by mundane standards. Besides achievements through one's career, finances, and loves, there are also those achieved through knowledge, moral standard, and character. Some people may not rise to high positions or make a fortune, but day in and day out, they volunteer in directing traffic for school children or assist those in need of their help in hospitals. They resolve to serve others and form broad connections with people. Can we say that their achievements are insignificant or their standing is low? From a mundane point of view, their achievements may seem limited, but their character is superior, for it is through their ordinariness that we can appreciate their greatness.

How to Work with People

If we want to accomplish anything in this world, we must know how to handle situations, how to use money, and especially, how to work with people's talents. Those who know how to do so may not be capable themselves, but since they know how to employ the skills of others, they can still benefit humanity and further social welfare. The following are four points on how best to work with people.

1. We must have an amiable attitude. When we greet others with a kind expression, we will promote harmony in human relationships. However, if as supervisors, we are always alienating others with our arrogance and authority, we will certainly not win the support or friendship of our subordinates. This is the age of democracy. Even presidents go to town hall meetings to hear the views at the grass-root level. They have to display their concern for the average citizen in order to gain his or her support. Similarly, if we want to gain the acceptance and love of our subordinates in the corporate office, the most important thing we need is an amiable attitude. People will find us approachable with our even-temperedness, which is conducive to enhancing communication at work.

2. We must have a humble mind. "Arrogance brings harm; humility brings benefit." If we can be more humble, we will gain the respect of others because "those who respect others will earn their respect in return." What we should avoid is being an empty vessel that makes the most noise. As the saying goes, "The more wheat ripens, the more their stalks bend." Therefore, a successful and wonderful supervisor will treat his or her subordinates with humility and broadmindedness.

3. We must be willing to accept advice. Some supervisors

tend to be authoritarian and make decisions based only on their own views. They do not allow others to air their opinions. When others speak, they will easily dismiss their views, showing no tolerance for the opinion of others. In reality, a good supervisor will listen to his or her employees, encouraging their voices and praising their ideas. Moreover, he will discern sound advice and follow it accordingly. When supervisors accept ideas from below, the intentions from above can also be passed down and accepted by everyone.

4. We must have the capacity to tolerate others. The ancients said, "One can row a boat inside a prime minister." Actually, it is more than just ministers who need to have the capacity to tolerate others. This aphorism applies to all of us too, because how promising a person's career can be hinges on how much that individual can tolerate. Moreover, how good a person's human relationships are also depends on his or her tolerance. Therefore, as supervisors, we must have the capacity to tolerate others in order to mingle well with our subordinates, like milk and water, so as to gain their support.

People have both strengths and shortcomings. As long as we know how to make use of their strengths, even brittle metal can be forged into steel. The keys in making use of the talents of others not only apply at work but also in the family between parents and children or between siblings. People who are doing well in their career, either in very large businesses or in politics, need to be skillful in employing the skills of their employees or subordinates. There are many methods available. Besides cherishing the talents of others and using them appropriately, we ourselves need to be well-cultivated in our morals so those working for us will respect and admire us. According to the saying, "Knowing how to read people is not as good as knowing how to use them well. Knowing how to use people well is not as good as knowing how to conduct ourselves."

Four Keys to Treating Others

People often have to play different roles at the same time, such as being both parent and child, both subordinate and supervisor, both teacher and friend, or even both lover and enemy. No matter which role we are playing, we need to treat others with sincerity, righteousness, magnanimity, and tolerance. The following are four key ways to treat others.

1. Treat our loved ones with a true heart. We may have many people we love and care for in this world such as our parents, spouse, children, siblings, and friends. They may even include our rulers and superiors. If they are people we respect and love, what can we offer them? We need to offer them a true heart. While money is very important in this world, it is not all-powerful. Money may be able to buy people but not a true heart. Therefore, if we want others to treat us with a true heart, we must first treat them with sincerity and trust, because if we are false and hypocritical towards them, they will not reciprocate with candor. Hence, treating others with a true heart is the first rule.

2. Treat our friends with righteousness. Do you have good friends? How do you treat them? Good friends are not merely for financial benefit, even though friends sometimes feel obliged to help in money matters. More importantly, friends are precious in giving each other guidance and advice. We should be like a mirror for one another, and provide support as necessary. When friends are in trouble, we may be able to sacrifice ourselves and give all we have out of our sense of loyalty and righteousness, in order to help them. However, if we are brave in counseling them and guiding them on a path of

virtue in ordinary times, it is something even more virtuous. Therefore, in treating friends, righteousness is of prime importance as it is far more valuable than money.

3. Treat our subordinates with magnanimity. As supervisors, we must provide our subordinates with positive causes and conditions, a pleasant countenance, compassion, and support. Supervisors should never act condescendingly and haughtily towards those working for them. They must treat their workers with magnanimity. For instance, when the latter speak inappropriately, we should tolerate them or when they make mistakes, we should forgive them. People junior to us are still learning because they started later than we did. If we fail to tolerate or teach them, we should feel ashamed for being someone with seniority. Therefore, as seniors or supervisors, we must have the magnanimity to promote junior workers and never be jealous of them or sabotage their efforts. These are the best ways to support them and contribute to their personal and professional growth.

4. Treat our enemies with tolerance. We may have various kinds of enemies, such as competitors in commerce, people holding opposing views in politics, or coworkers seeking to obstruct or sabotage us at work. In facing different situations, gains, losses, and people with conflicting views, we must have the tolerance to embrace them and work with all of them. If we are able to transform an enemy into a friend with our tolerance, we will have one less enemy and gain one more friend. He or she might even be able to help us in our career in the future. Therefore, we need to treat our enemies with tolerance.

Tangible wealth is limited, and money cannot resolve all problems, for it cannot bring real loving-kindness. However, if we treat people with compassion, they will always remember us.

How to Treat People Positively

We all need to connect with people every day. When we interact with people, we have to decide how to treat them, and there are many ways to do so. Some people are strict, aloof, heartless, or selfish in treating others. Naturally, they will not win the love of those around them. In conducting ourselves, we must instead be considerate of others in everything we do. We should be positive in every way in order to bring harmony in human relationships. The following are keys to treating people positively.

1. We should be more understanding and less presumptuous. In getting along with one another, we should speak out clearly on every matter. We should not harbor ill feelings bred out of suspicion. Therefore, when a situation occurs with our friends, neighbors, relatives, or coworkers, we should be open and honest in talking about it. We need to put ourselves in others' shoes in order to appreciate their point of view, instead of misunderstanding or being presumptuous of that person. Some people often make assumptions about the possible ill intentions or harmful ideas other people may have. Such a negative and presumptuous attitude is something we should refrain from in human relationships.

2. We should be more forgiving and less hostile. We need to treat people with tolerance and forgiveness, and not harbor bad feelings toward them. When we are hostile toward others, they will naturally reciprocate in a similar manner. If we are more forgiving and understanding towards the people around us, we will win more friendships over time. However, if we are narrow-minded and unforgiving, we will naturally find it difficult to gain true friends.

3. We should be more attentive and less suspicious. We need to tend to people's needs and appreciate their joys and troubles, so that we can provide assistance and consolation appropriately. When they are joyous, we should offer our blessings with a sincere heart that shares in their happiness. They will be able to feel our warmth and be moved by our caring. We should never suspect them at every turn and be prejudiced in our thinking, nor make negative assumptions. Otherwise, we will not win their trust because if we want to work with them, we should not be suspicious.

4. We should be more tolerant and less dismissive. In conducting ourselves, we must be tolerant because the scale of our achievements hinges on the capacity of our mind. Over the ages, many people have been able to achieve major accomplishments because of their large capacity to tolerate others.

During the Period of the Warring States, four wise men were able to widely attract the talents of the time and assembled a team of three thousand people whom they could make the best use of without having to dismiss a single one of them. The number of people available to work for us will be the same number of people our mind can contain. When we can tolerate others, they will do the same in return, allowing us to bring our talents and skills into full play. On the contrary, if we dismiss them outright, they will not include us in what they do. Then, no matter how talented or skilled we may be, we will not be able to put them to good use and will just end up being a fool.

Interacting with people is like looking into a mirror. When we treat others well, they will repay us with kindness. If we are mean, we will not win any hearts. Therefore, we must be positive in thinking about and treating others in every matter. As such, we will end up with positive results.

The Way of Treating Guests

We often have friends and relatives visiting us at home, or clients and business contacts coming to our workplace. In temples, lay devotees, monastics from other temples, and people from all walks of life, visit on a daily basis. Therefore, the monastic in charge of reception and hospitality is very important. In Chinese, such a monastic is called "*zhikeshi*," which means one who appreciates the needs of guests and the ways to treat them. Whether it is at a temple, company or within one's family, everyone should know how to receive visitors. The following are four tips for consideration:

1. Make guests who are friends feel at home. According to the saying, "When we have friends visiting from afar, we are truly overjoyed." So when friends who have been out of touch for a long time come by on short notice, we should not let them feel uncomfortable or treat them like strangers. We should be hospitable and receive them with enthusiasm, so they will feel at home. Once they arrive, we should treat them with the best courtesy by offering them tea, a good meal, and an opportunity to relax. After the meal is prepared, a host should come out of the kitchen quickly and greet the guests at the dinner table. A good host should not still be sweeping the floor or making tea by the time the guests arrive.

2. Assist guests who have problems by solving their difficulties. According to two popular Chinese sayings, "Every day is easy when staying home; everything becomes difficult when traveling," and "One relies on parents at home and friends when away." People inevitably come across difficulties. When we have guests who are in trouble, whether they are business associates, former coworkers, supervisors from work, or

even just friends, we should show them genuine care. We cannot hem and haw giving them the impression that we are trying to avoid them. It is best if we try to solve their problems directly. Otherwise, we can provide ideas, empathetic listening, or other sources of assistance. All in all, we have to help them so that they will not find the visit a waste of time. This is an important way to treat guests with difficulties.

3. Offer joy and hope to guests who are just dropping by. Some people visit without any special purpose. They just drop by in the spur of the moment without any prior notice. However, we still have to treat them well, giving them joy and satisfaction so they will feel the warmth of human sentiments and have hope for life. Such is the way to treat guests.

4. In treating guests in high positions, we should conduct ourselves appropriately without being arrogant or self-effacing. While we treat guests with respect and courtesy, there is a still a clear line between host and guest. For instance, in holding a meeting, the chair, delegates, and members are the hosts. So even when officials of high status attend the meeting, they are only there as guests. When the president of a big country visits a small country, he or she becomes the guest of honor of the latter. Similarly, the president of the small country will also be the guest of honor when visiting the big country. The assigned roles for host and guest apply equally regardless of how important a person is. Therefore, while some guests may enjoy a very high status, they still have to follow the host's wishes and not take over as host. As host, we should behave appropriately without being arrogant or self-effacing, in order to play our role well.

These are the generally accepted rules or conventions for being a host or guest. As a good host, we must know how to treat guests appropriately.

Cultivation in Treating People

People have different minds, natures, behaviors, and morals. In terms of personal cultivation, some are wise and others undeveloped. In terms of age, there are seniors and juniors. In terms of capabilities and ethics, there are the intelligent, the foolish, the sagely, and the common. How do we treat people who can be so different? We need to pay attention to the following admonitions in order to develop our own cultivation in treating others.

1. It is difficult to treat mean people without hate. Consider the following descriptions: "The minds of mean people are selfish and malicious," "the mean only want what they can enjoy and profit from," and "the mean want people to be the same as them." Just the facial expressions of these people alone can arouse dislike and unpleasantness. It is certainly easy to hate them, because their behavior is sometimes even more shameless than evildoers. They are selfish and good at flattering others in order to manipulate situations for their own personal gain. Mean people are also typical fence-sitters, watching which way the wind blows. While they may appear sincere and loyal towards others, they are already scheming in their hearts to harm people. That is why there is the saying, "One is better off offending a person of morals than neglecting a mean person." It is truly difficult not to get angry at or hate them. Therefore, when we come across mean people, we have to pay attention and be cautious so that we do not offend them inadvertently and bring endless trouble upon ourselves.

2. It is difficult to treat the wise with the proper courtesy. In contrast to the mean, "the wise hold a just and forgiving mind"; "they learn from those who are virtuous, and

treat everyone as if they were their own loved ones." Furthermore, the wise also "wish for others to emulate them." They are courteous to all and deferential to the capable, treating people with warmth and equality. They are low-key in whatever they do and do not like to publicize their merits. Even if they are humiliated by others, they are not bothered. Therefore, most people neglect proper courtesy in dealing with them, thinking that since they are people of high morals, there is no need to adhere to etiquette. The truth is, while the wise do not seek anything from others, we must offer them the proper courtesy, since even in treating ordinary people, we have to be proper and polite.

3. It is difficult to treat subordinates with a smiling face. To maintain personal and social order, we need to differentiate between the young and the old, seniors and juniors. However, we should never take this as a standard for social status. For instance, we may find it difficult to be kind and pleasant to people who are younger in age, lower in position, junior in rank, and inferior in capability. We may have trouble treating them with warmth and consideration. Moreover, if we see someone who is not as learned as we are or worse off financially, we will become arrogant and look down on such a person. While a position may be high or low, every person enjoys an equal sense of dignity. Therefore, we need to be hospitable and treat everyone equally.

4. It is easy to fawn when dealing with our superiors. While water flows downwards, people tend to climb upwards; this is the natural course for all things and people. It is our nature as humans to seek to progress and reach higher levels. Nowadays, however, young people just want to go straight to the top. They latch on to the rich and famous thinking that this is the way to make it. It is very difficult for them not to flatter and fawn when-

ever they meet someone of high status.

According to the saying, "The extent of one's knowledge is clear for people to see, for there is no way to pretend. However, with practice, it is easy to fake a foot for a mile." This only shows how difficult it is to have definite standards for ethical cultivation. However, the above admonitions clearly point to the core of human weakness.

The Four Don'ts in Treating People

Of the people we keep in touch with regularly or friends we see only occasionally, some are as pleasant as the spring breezes, and so everyone wants to be around them. However, there are also those who instill fear in others because their behavior or mood is unacceptable. Worse still, some of them are so unpleasant that after meeting them once, no one wants to ever see them again. In life, we all want others to think well of us, and not treat us with anger or hatred. But if we intend to make a good impression, we need to pay attention to our attitude of treating people. The following are the four "don'ts" we have to consider when relating to people.

1. Don't look for a payback; be compassionate and caring. Praise or flattery cannot be compared to the care and support people give us when we are suffering or in pain. Therefore, we should generously give our compassion and care to others. However, "In giving, we do not speak about it; in receiving, we do not forget." When others help us, we need to repay their kindness a hundredfold. If we give others some assistance, we should not be looking for a payback. Moreover, we should not even keep it in mind. When anyone looks for a payback in giving, such a person will be viewed as a publicity seeker who wants a good name. When we are able to give without any concern for profit, we are then truly compassionate.

2. Don't bear any anger or hatred; be tolerant and yielding. The greatest cultivation in life is tolerance. When we treat others with an open mind and a big heart, we will be able to forgive and tolerate any transgression with compassion and understanding. Naturally, no anger or hatred will arise, and we will not be full of complaints. When

we are able to hold fewer grudges, life can be easily fulfilled.

3. Don't be attached to ignorance; make the right choice.
   According to the sutras, "Phenomena are neither good
   nor bad in themselves; standards for right or wrong
   should be the guiding principle." It is also said, "Worry
   and suffering are the result of delusion and fabrication."
   According to the Buddha's teachings of the transcenden-
   tal Dharma, all phenomena are "without cessation and
   without arising, without division and without unity of
   meaning, without end and without permanence, and without coming and without going." However, from the
   mundane point of view, everything is either major or
   minor, good or bad, serious or light, kind or harmful.
   Therefore, we need to be able to make a choice as to what
   we can do and what we cannot and should not do. When
   we are clear in our reasoning, we can assess the gravity
   of any matter and the right and wrong of it. We will then
   be able to judge what is kind or harmful. This is the
   meaning of wisdom, for without it, we are ignorant and
   deluded. By being reasonable, we can tell right from
   wrong, and with wisdom, we can differentiate kindness
   from harm. We all need to know the differences between
   them.

4. Don't be arrogant; be humble and gentle. In conducting
   ourselves, it is our duty to be respectful towards our seniors, and act with gentle kindness towards our peers.
   When we are humble and respectful, we will give others
   the impression of gentleness, courtesy, compassion, and
   kindness. They will be happy and eager to get close to
   us. Therefore, if we treat others with humility and gentleness, we can naturally make broad connections with
   people.

The cardinal rule in dealing with people and handling matters is forgiveness, which we should apply to both self and others. In our everyday life, we should not take the shortcomings of others as mistakes. Instead, we should always have the intent to make a positive connection, as opposed to making enemies. We should be tolerant and patient in winning people over, and when the time is right, we will be able to earn their respect. Therefore, we need to bear in mind the four "don'ts" in life.

The Way to Being Carefree

People do not want to be bound by anything and wish to live in freedom and be at ease. However, we do not gain freedom just by wishing for it. In our everyday life, we are often bound by the fetters of fame and fortune, burdened by troubles and worry, and constrained by the right and wrong, gains and losses between self and others. How can we gain peace and ease? "Being bound" is not necessarily the result of external circumstances or other people. It comes from within our own minds, for we bind ourselves. Therefore, the real question is how we can liberate ourselves. The following are some of the ways to consider:

1. Let go of honor and disgrace. Honor is something everyone seeks. However, some people end up disgracing themselves in the pursuit of glory. Others may indulge in their momentary glory and achieve nothing in the end. Therefore, when honor arrives, we should not be swayed by it. Do not be overjoyed with honor or be depressed in disgrace. We have to let go of both honor and disgrace, for how else can we find peace? When we are able to let "what is honorable be honored and disgraceful be disgraced," setting our own standards for good or bad and not be influenced by external circumstances, we will then be able to become carefree.

2. Let go of fame and fortune. It is human nature to seek fame and fortune, and there is nothing wrong with pursuing them in moderation. However, if the focus of our life is only on fame and fortune, we will find ourselves bound by them. For instance, we might watch the stock market closely every day with our every emotion hanging on the rise and fall of stock prices. Worse still, we may be busying ourselves all day long, latching onto others to curry favors with the hope of making big

money and gaining celebrity status. The result, unfortunately, may not always be success in either, as we only end up being bound by the fetters of fame and fortune. Therefore, we need to let go of them both in order to live a carefree life.

3. Let go of gain and loss. Life is full of gains and losses. Yet in terms of the two, we often lose something in what we gain and gain something in what we lose. They are no absolute categories. However, some people take them too seriously and start calculating and bickering over them. They find it hard to accept even a small disadvantage, and at the same time are not necessarily happy at gaining something. In the end, they keep adding to their burden all the time and carry an intangible but heavy load due to their concern over gain and loss. Consequently, in seeking spiritual liberation, we must let go of our attachment to gain and loss.

4. Let go of our desires. In our daily lives, we can hardly depart from the pursuit of the five desires for money, sex, fame, food, and sleep. In order to satisfy our desires, we work hard every day running this way and that. However, desires are like a bottomless pit which cannot be filled. Therefore, people often become slaves to their desires without even realizing it. They weigh themselves down with numerous matters because of their cravings. It is only by letting go of our greediness for self-gratification that we can unload the burden of our mind and thereby gain peace and comfort.

What does a liberated person do? Such a person knows when and how to let go! What does a carefree person do? Such an individual simply lets go! When we let go of the load weighing upon our heart, we can be liberated. Like a suitcase, we pick it up when we need it, and when we no longer have use for it, we put it away. If we carry it with us all the time, it will become a burden.

Look Back and Think

In life, we have half the world in front of us and the other half behind us. Most people can only see what is in front and not behind them. Therefore, they fight with others every day in the front half of the world until they are tired, battered, and bleeding. In reality, if we look back and think, our vistas will be much broader and our world more open. "Look back and think" embodies this philosophy of life as explained below.

1. It is better to be slow than glib in arguing. The greatest cultivation in life is not fighting with others. Some people like to argue and debate. They always want to get the upper hand and win an argument. In reality, the truth is not gained in being loud or applying intellectual manipulation. If something is unreasonable, it does not matter how articulate people are in arguing, because the truth will not be on their side. On the other hand, those who are slow in speech tend not to fight with others, and people will find them understanding and reasonable. Therefore, being slow in speech actually makes it easier to express our reasoning.

2. It is better to be reticent than talkative. As the saying goes, "Talking too much is not as good as doing a lot." Talking too much often means we speak when we should not or say the wrong things. There are people who like to talk, and while others say a few words, they tend to speak ten or twenty times as much. They may even carry on for twenty minutes nonstop. The truth is we make mistakes when we say too much. Being talkative not only earns the dislike of others, but also results in resentment. The ancients treasured their words like gold. The sayings "Silence is golden," and "There is no danger as

serious as talking too much" are certainly words of wisdom.

3. It is better to wait for an opportunity than to move rashly. *Humble Table, Wise Fare* states, "No deluded thinking in the mind, no inappropriate action of the body, and no improper speech from the mouth. The wise gain integrity this way." Some people like to show off and stand out in a group. They often cannot wait for the proper conditions to be in place, and instead start to act ahead of time. As a result, they only find themselves failing in their efforts. It is like singing, for if we are one beat ahead, we may go out of tune. Therefore, we should wait for the right opportunity and conditions, and not act rashly when the timing is off. Otherwise, we will find ourselves just missing success and, as a result, wasting all our previous efforts. This means we should never move rashly, but act only when a good reason presents itself.

4. It is better to be organized than chaotic. "With planning there will be no chaos; with job division there will be no rush." Some people are unorganized in their work and get busy for no good reason; some follow others in a mad rush. Worse still, the more some people try and help, the busier things get. We should, however, be clear in our thinking and skillful at work and the way we conduct ourselves. No matter how many things we are handling or how busy and chaotic the situation is, we should be organized. Order can be found within the chaos of anything we do. We must never run around blindly, accomplishing little in spite of our efforts. In this way we lose the opportunity to learn from our work.

"Look back and think" is reverse psychology. It allows us to transcend our original frame of mind and expand our world.

Be Mindful of What Lies Ahead

"Even if people have no distant concerns, there will certainly be worries close at hand." Not only do we need to look far and high, but we must also prepare for what lies ahead. We should see clearly what the future holds, as well as a way out of trouble. We should leave sufficient room in whatever we do, so that there will be space for us to turn around if necessary. Therefore, to be mindful of what lies ahead is an important guideline in life.

1. Be prepared for a rainy day. A Chinese motto goes, "One should be prepared before the rain comes and not dig a well after we have become thirsty." If we are prepared for anything, we need not worry. We need to anticipate a day of "not having" in times of "having." Thus, we should always have umbrellas ready in case winds and clouds gather in the sky. We need to store up enough food in the fall so we can survive the winter. Having a flashlight handy by day, we need not worry about darkness at night. While we may not be able to counter natural disasters completely, we can still be prepared in advance to minimize the damage. Therefore, we have to anticipate danger in times of peace. Being prepared for a rainy day is the right attitude towards life.

2. Think of getting off stage when we are still on it. All good things must come to an end, and there is no show which does not close. When a show is finished, its actors must get off stage after the curtain call. After a speech is delivered and its ideas expressed, the speaker must bow and leave. Therefore, when one gets on stage, getting off is inevitable. It is a law of nature. However, some people do not appreciate this truth. It is easy for them to get on but difficult to leave. High officials who

gain power may bring much glory and benefit to everyone associated with them. But how should they conduct themselves once they lose their position and power? We should, therefore, think of the day we must leave while we are still up at the top. We should never be arrogant when we have power and create enemies by staying too long, because very simply, we need to think about getting off stage while we are still on it.

3. Be mindful of the lows when we are riding high. Prosperity, decline, glory, and humiliation are all part of life. These are the stages that we go through during our life. Some people do well at a young age and make a lot of money. They may be very talented, enjoy excellent human relationships, and have every door open for them wherever they go. However, we need to bear in mind that impermanence is the rule of life. Just as the moon waxes and wanes, life goes through birth, old age, sickness, and death. All things in the world cannot escape the cycle of existence, abidance, decay, and extinction. When we are flying high and basking in glory, have we ever thought of what we will do if we fail and suffer? Thus, we should prepare ourselves well ahead of time. A wily rabbit has three burrows, ants store food for winter, and bees make honey in a timely fashion. How can people not have a sense of imminent danger? Therefore, we need to be mindful of the lows when we are riding high.

4. Bear in mind setbacks in times of success. The tide rises and falls; life is smooth as well as difficult. When we face setbacks, we naturally need to understand what leads to success, but when we live in success, what do we do if difficulties suddenly appear? It is said, "When we are doing well, we need to prepare an alternative route, then there will be no fear in good times. When we are faced with failure, we must find a way out so that we can survive hardships." Therefore, life can be smooth or diffi-

cult, but it is only by leaving things behind and following positive conditions that we can find a way out.

All in all, in anything we do, we succeed if we are prepared
and fail if we are not. When we are aware of what lies ahead, we
will be spared from losing control and being thrown into fear when
we face difficult situations.

Learning from the Wise and Capable

The wise and capable have distinct characteristics. Most of those who are wise and capable are usually a grade above others in wisdom, and their morals and character are also superior to that of others as well. The following are four things we can learn from such people:

1. Do not be arrogant in a high position. "A country with integrity ennobles their ministers; a family of riches breeds arrogant children." It is rare and worthy of respect for a person to remain humble and modest on gaining fame, fortune, power, and status. It is a common flaw of people to be arrogant because of their talents, special endowments, public position, or wealth. Looking back on the numerous kings and emperors throughout the ages, some might have owned enormous wealth and impressed everyone with their prowess. However, if they were arrogant, lacked ethics, and failed to protect and cherish their subjects, they usually ended up being overthrown by their countrymen. Thus, arrogance will inevitably lead to failure. Only by being humble when one has power and fortune can one gain the support of others.

2. Do not betray common values in victory. The greatest victory in life is not defeating the enemy but our own ego. We might be breezing along in business, making huge sums in manufacturing, rising high in politics, or riding the crest of our personal reputation. However, no matter how great the victory or success, it cannot prevail over the natural course of action and reason. We can only have true victory when it is gained under acceptable and reasonable social and personal circumstances. Therefore,

we should not act contrary to all established values even when we gain victory. In fact, we need to rid ourselves of this mindset of winning and losing, in order to live without conflicts and gain a life of harmony.

3. Be humble and wise. Over the ages, the wise, sagely, and capable rulers mostly treated others with humility and courtesy in order to gain the support of those with ability and moral standing. With the help of wise and intelligent aides, those in power were able to complete their mission and gain a good name in history. On the other hand, if they had chosen to act aloof and stay on their perch at the top, they would only have succeeded in instilling fear in others. Thus, they would not have benefited from favorable conditions nor succeeded in their career, revealing as well a flaw in their moral character.

4. Be tolerant and upright. It is good to be righteous and upright in character. However, it is even better to be both upright and gentle. Being gentle, we have tolerance and will be better equipped to face the difficulties and setbacks in life. We will be able to retreat from any situation without causing harm to ourselves. Since "a sharp knife cuts easily," by being too tough and inflexible, we may find ourselves failing before the battle even starts. Therefore, we need to be cautious.

The experience and wisdom of our predecessors are precious guidelines for us. Nowadays, there are many publications on management science, finance, and even the science of leadership. In reality, learning from the wise and capable is much more important.

The State of the Virtuous Sages

Over the ages, people have greatly admired the virtuous sages. As the saying goes, "We admire the high mountains, and while we may not be able to reach their heights, we aspire to be there!" The state of the virtuous sages is above and beyond the material world, but at the same time, they never depart from humanity. They include the universe and nature in their cultivation and use their superior character to teach people and influence the world. The following are four similes that explain what the virtuous sages are like:

1. Like a clear mirror and still water reflecting the mind. When their mind is as clear and calm as still water, they will not be moved easily by external conditions. However, "still water" is not "dead water," but more like a polished mirror that can reflect clearly in order to make manifest the true appearance and intent. In addition, they will be able to see through what is behind every situation, allowing them to know when and how to advance and retreat. Therefore, the mind of virtuous sages has no attachments and will not give rise to discrimination against anything. At the same time, they are always mindful of all sentient beings.

2. Like the tall and imposing Mt. Tai in cultivating their character. The virtuous sages do not seek to establish themselves in high positions. They apply their value in life by exerting their moral influence upon others, the way "grass bends as the wind blows." They are less worried about not having a position, but instead are more concerned about what they can establish themselves with. Therefore, the virtuous sages resolve to be like the high and imposing Mt. Tai, wishing their moral influence

to be just as lofty. Such is how the virtuous sages establish themselves in life.

3. Like the blue sky and radiant sun in dealing with matters. The virtuous sages deal with matters based on the principle of benefiting humanity. They focus on what should be done with little concern about the criticism of others. More importantly, they do not care about personal gain or loss, and will not hesitate even if they have to sacrifice their life. Courageous and enthusiastic Chinese heroes like the Song General Yue Fei vowed to "repay their country with unreserved loyalty." They faced the world with an open heart as bright as the blue sky and the shining sun. That is why their spirit has lasted through the ages inspiring great reverence.

4. Like the light breeze and bright moon in treating people. The virtuous sages treat others with sincerity and honesty, for they are not arrogant or opinionated. They uphold the four principles of not holding onto suspicion and jealousy, not persisting in their views, not refusing to make changes, and not being self-centered. Therefore, the heart of the virtuous sages is broad and open like the light breeze and bright moon shining clearly in the sky, free on any clouds.

The virtuous sages consider the whole universe and humanity as their teacher. As we learn from them, we are able to gain strength from all their goodness.

A Noble Character

There is a saying, "When people have no cravings, they will naturally have noble character." A person does not receive the respect and consideration of others because of his or her academic achievements, capabilities, riches or status, but rather is honored for his or her character. Therefore, having noble character is more important than having knowledge or money, for it is the intangible wealth of person. The following are keys for how to cultivate noble character:

1. We must not turn against our principles because of momentary poverty. For instance, in renouncing our home life to become a monastic, we cannot lose our resolve for the Way and give up our vows because of poverty and hardship. Likewise, a woman should never sell her body because of poverty; otherwise, she is giving herself up to shamelessness at the expense of all her self-respect. According to an ancient Chinese saying, "Scholars would rather starve than sell their books; warriors would rather starve than sell their swords." Therefore, we should never turn against our principles because of hardship or a lack of money. We must persevere for the sake of our mission and principles.

2. We should not change our path and resolve because of poverty. For instance, we may be a righteous person, but we choose to follow the bad examples of others by engaging in criminal acts. We may have vowed to practice benevolence and generosity at an earlier time, but because we have become poor, we give up on our practice entirely. In reality, even though we have no money or any power, we still have a heart and mind, and while we may have nothing at all, we still have a mouth. We

can generate kind thoughts and speak well of others as a form of giving. When we are able to face poverty and remain unchanged, we can live a simple life with little or no craving for fame and fortune. On the other hand, if we are shameless, we will inevitably sink further into poverty. Therefore, we should rather die in poverty and keep to our path than to live in wealth without our principles. Being able to persevere in poverty without changing our resolve will certainly win the respect of others.

3. We should not give up in the face of difficulties. When life gets tough, we have to face it. We must not give up our responsibilities and ideals in life because of hardship. Nowadays, many young people are filled with ideals and dreams for the future, and so they make vows to succeed while still in school. However, once they enter society and encounter some minor difficulty, they retreat, refuse to progress, and give up their ideals, because their resolve was not firm enough. A person needs strong resolve and willpower in order to withstand the test of adversity.

4. We must not turn back in hardship. Everybody suffers one way or another. When faced with hardship, we need to analyze the situation with a cool head and break through our attachments. It is only when we resolve to overcome our difficulties that we may encounter good opportunities. Throughout the ages, there have been numerous heroes, kings, and generals who succeeded in whatever they did. All of them gained success by overcoming hardship and adversity. They were able to strengthen their resolve in the struggle and succeed in their endeavors in the end. Therefore, if we are able to overcome difficulties, we can turn the situation around. When we can solve a problem, we can resolve a crisis. If we are not afraid of our difficulties, we will learn to make the best use of timing to gain success. However, if

we are easily turned back by minor difficulties, we will never be able to attain our goals or fulfill our vows.

"Rome was not built in one day." When we work hard, strive on, contribute and sacrifice, we will be able to stand up again from failures and setbacks. Our success and our character will forever win the respect of others.

How to Shoulder Responsibility

Success is the culmination of a series of experiences. We should be brave in shouldering responsibility and be willing to give in order to stand out. To cultivate the strength to shoulder responsibility, we need to start with knowing and training ourselves. We cannot hide from our shortcomings or be afraid to speak about them. By facing our shortcomings, we can progress and improve. The ways to shoulder responsibility are as follows:

1. Do not shirk responsibility in any matter. The worst problem in working with people arises when they shirk responsibility. If they are only interested in claiming credit and not admitting any fault, no one will want to work with them. Some people never want to shoulder any responsibility. People like that are limited in what they can achieve. The best attitude in work is having the courage to take on any responsibility that is imminent. Most capable people have the strength to do so, and their superiors will give them major duties and projects to work on more often. When they have more opportunities to take on serious assignments, it is only natural that they will have outstanding achievements.

2. Do not act like a bureaucrat when dealing with people. It is inevitable that we will face the general public at one point or another in whatever we do. In dealing with the people, we must be humble, courteous, and respectful in order to win their support. Some people like to speak and act bureaucratically. They not only fail to provide support for others when required, but enjoy making things difficult for them. They lack the cultivation to treat others with kindness and are actually exposing their own inabilities by acting this way. Therefore, people with the strength to shoulder responsibility never act

bureaucratically towards others.

3. Do not slack off in personal cultivation. If we want to achieve something in life, aside from cultivating favorable conditions, it is most important to be healthy and positive ourselves. For instance, we need to be knowledgeable, farsighted, and both physically and mentally healthy. We also should keep a proper schedule for work and rest every day. More importantly, we need to be progressive in our endeavors and have the willpower and perseverance to strive on. We must maintain optimism in our effort and never slack off, retreat, shrink back, or become listless in what we do. Thus, we will gain the ability, spirit, and physical strength to shoulder responsibility.

4. Do not complain about your superiors. Those who are in charge of an organization should be able to take any blame or complaint. They should be encompassing like the good earth, which nurtures grain, springs forth rivers, allows people to walk upon it, putting up with everything in silence. As for people who are subordinates, they should have as much tolerance as their superiors. They should be willing to take on more responsibility and accept any disadvantage, because their bosses will appreciate them for their efforts. If, on the contrary, we as subordinates are always complaining, our superiors will naturally think little of us, and be reluctant to provide us with any opportunity for promotion. So, how do we get along with our supervisors? The most important thing is not to complain, but use the cultivation of the earth as our model.

Whether we are capable of shouldering responsibility or not depends on how good we are in our practice of cultivation. If we are perfectly willing to accept any disadvantage, allowing others to make use of us while remaining content in any adversity, we will be able to cultivate a tolerance for any situation between heaven and earth, as well as between friends and enemies.

Character Building

We all wish to have good character, because with good character we can be a good person. How do we achieve good character? The following are some guidelines:

1. Base wealth on "no greed." In order to have good character, we must first rid ourselves of strong cravings and greed. Greed can never be satisfied. The following passage illustrates greed. "Now that I have many acres of fertile land, I want a government title to impress others. I do not want to start at the bottom of the ladder, nor even in the middle. When I am at the top rung, I want to be the emperor for a while. When I am the emperor and everything is going well, I long to live forever." Money and material goods in the world are limited, but people's cravings are limitless! No matter how rich a greedy person may be, such a person is still poor. Only when we find joy in contentment and live a life of simple means can we be truly wealthy. Therefore, greediness is poverty and having no greed is wealth.

2. Base nobility on "no need." "When people covet nothing, they gain a noble character." People often degrade themselves in trying to satisfy their strong cravings for material wealth, and insist on fulfilling their many needs and wants. If we are greedy and never content with what we have, we will always be asking people for favors everywhere we go. We will end up being shameless in our efforts, as we flatter and scheme for more. But if on the contrary, we do not covet fame and fortune, our character will naturally be ennobled.

3. Base harmony on "no anger." The sutras teach, "The fire of anger can burn a forest of merits." Anger is like fire.

Once anger arises, it can spread like wildfire, making us feel hot and uncomfortable. When the fire of our anger burns from within, we get upset and unhappy. In the heat of anger, we will ignore the ethical standards and human sentiments we uphold. As a result, not only are we unhappy, but we also end up compromising our character. Only when we put out the flames of anger and treat others with forgiveness and compassion can we achieve calmness and tranquility in our hearts. In this way, we will then be able to gain peace and harmony.

4. Base wisdom on "no delusion." According to the saying, "One would rather fight with an intelligent person than speak with an ignorant one." People are deluded because of ignorance, wrongheaded views, and the lack of reasoning. It is often uncomfortable speaking with deluded people, because they are inflexible and cannot reason, and any reasoning they may have is always half-baked. Ignorance can be frightening, because it reflects wrongheaded thinking. When we are without delusion and ignorance, we gain wisdom; without delusion and ignorance, we gain equanimity and ease.

People are sometimes called the most advanced beings because of their self-respect; while self-respect comes from having good character. Our character is not given to us by our parents or teachers, nor can it be bought with any amount of gold or money. It is cultivated according to morals and ethics, and refined by understanding the truth. Some people leave behind a good reputation spanning centuries, while others gain a bad name for themselves for millennia. The difference between the two depends on having good character.

Four Kinds of Mind

We all have a mind. However, if we do not look after it well, then it can transform into many unwholesome states. For instance, the mind can be ignorant, angry, jealous, pessimistic, depressed, passive, and hopeless. Buddhism teaches that the mind is like a craftsman or a painter that can create various pieces of artwork. It can change for the better or worse. The four kinds of human mind include the compassionate, the wise, the reasonable, and the greedy, which are defined as follows:

1. Compassion is the mind of mercy. Do you have a compassionate mind? The only thing a person cannot do without is compassion. Some people may be cheated out of their life savings, and have their house taken away and all their valuables stolen. However, a compassionate mind cannot be stolen by anyone. Compassion is a mind of mercy that cares for others and has sympathy for all sentient beings. "Care for all aged just as we do our own; love the children of others as much as we love ours." This is compassion. When we witness the suffering of others as they go through sickness, old age, and death, we should have empathy for them. A single thought of compassion and caring will link us with the ways of the universe.

2. Understanding is the mind of discernment. Do you have an understanding mind? It is very important for us to appreciate the difference between benevolence and malice. Whatever benefits others is benevolence, and whatever causes harm to others is malice. Sometimes, we may do things that harm others as well as ourselves, which constitutes wrongdoing. However, if it is something that may not benefit ourselves but benefits others,

it is the most benevolent deed. If we can discern the difference between benevolence and harm, right and wrong, we have an understanding mind. If, on the other hand, we fail to tell the difference and cannot think clearly, we become ignorant and unwholesome.

3. Ignorance is the mind of greed and anger. Do you have a mind of ignorance? An ignorant mind holds wrongheaded views or thoughts. It manifests itself in our greed and anger, and leads us to act discourteously toward others. That is why others will consider us ignorant. Ignorant people do not understand the cause of any matter and only blame the results. That is being foolish and deluded indeed.

4. Wisdom is the mind of beauty. Do you have a mind of wisdom? People with wisdom can understand right from wrong, good from bad. They know how to judge for themselves in terms of what to give or take. That is wisdom. With wisdom, we can understand the reality of the universe, and as a result, know how to eradicate suffering. With wisdom, we will be able to appreciate the nature of emptiness in all things and live at ease.

The mind is like a factory. A good mind will manufacture good products while an unwholesome one will be the source of pollution. People have many kinds of mind. We can all adjust our mind and change an unwholesome mind into one of kindness and beauty. We need to understand ourselves and be in control, so that we can be our own master. Therefore, we need to know, understand, and differentiate the four kinds of mind, so that we will know where we are going in life.

How to Speak

Speech is an important means of communication. Within an organization, people who can speak appropriately and humorously will leave a deep impression in the minds of others. In getting along with people, speaking properly can enhance harmony in human relationships. The following tips explain how to speak well:

1. Speak joyous words of Chan. In our daily life, we need to speak words that give others joy so we can enhance human relationship. Words of Chan are speech with humor and wisdom. Within an organization, if we often speak joyous words of Chan, they can reduce the stress in any environment and increase happiness in life. They can help people relax and be at ease, while still engaged in a serious and demanding life. Therefore, we should say happy words of Chan often, encouraging others to enjoy talking with us.

2. Speak honest or truthful words. Confucius said, "Know what you know, and know what you don't know." In conducting ourselves, we have to be truthful in our speech so we can be open and at ease. If we lie, we will always be afraid of being discovered, and we will have no peace of mind. We will end up like the little shepherd who cried wolf. Over time, even if we speak the truth, nobody will believe us anymore. Therefore, in getting along with others, we need to speak truthfully or honestly in order to earn the trust of others.

3. Speak beautiful words of respect. In speaking, we should offer beautiful words that people enjoy hearing. We have to give people joy by what we say. How do we do it? Confucius said, "Enjoy speaking about the kind-

ness of others." Mencius also asserted, "Refrain from talking about the ills of others." We should speak words of praise for people's kind deeds, words of respect for their achievements, words of thanks for their service, and words of encouragement for their progress. When we speak, our words should give others joy and make them feel important. In return, they will also speak kind words to us. If not, it will be like that warning in the *Book of Rites* [*Li Ji*], "Putting forth negative speech begets negative words from others in return." Therefore, we need to speak respectful words.

4. Speak positive words that benefit others. The renowned Chinese military strategist Sunzi said, "Giving others beneficial words is more precious than pearls and jade; harming others with negative words is worse than being cut down by a sword." Before uttering any words, we should ask ourselves if what we are about to say will be of help to others. If what we say is not going to help others or may even cause them harm, it is better for us not to say anything. Words that do not benefit others may ruin their future and reputation. Worse still, they may throw people into the deep pit of suffering. In speaking therefore, we should say things that benefit others.

We all talk every day, but what should we say? Besides not saying harsh words, lies, nonsense, and divisive speech, we should in particular say things that benefit and respect others.

Levels of People

There are different levels of people. Which one do we belong to, and how do we differentiate the levels of people? The following are a few guidelines.

1. Top-level people have both compassion and wisdom. Are you a top-level person? Top-level people not only have compassion but also wisdom. Compassion is kind-heartedness that enables us to treat others with love and empathy, and provide them with assistance. With compassion and loving-kindness, we naturally want to give others joy and alleviate their suffering. When we have empathy for the pain and suffering of others, we want to help them and give them the joy to restore faith to their life. Such intentions and actions are the hallmarks of compassion. In addition, we need wisdom to be able to tell right from wrong or kindness from harm. With wisdom, we can teach and help others more effectively. Therefore, people with both compassion and wisdom are at the top-level.

2. Medium-level people have compassion but no wisdom. Such people have a loving heart. However, they lack wisdom and cannot truly appreciate the realities of good or bad, kindness or harm, right or wrong, righteousness or deceitfulness. They do not have good reasoning or understanding of matters. Even though they may not understand the rationale of things very well, they often accept disadvantages in treating others with compassion and loving-kindness. As such, they can still be considered very good people; therefore, they belong to the medium-level.

3. Low-level people have intelligence but no compassion.

There are some very intelligent people who border on being manipulative and untrustworthy. They have no compassion with their high intelligence. If asked for assistance, they do not want to contribute anything. When needed for support, they choose to fold their arms and watch from the sidelines. People like that are very clever, but they do not like to make connections with others or offer help. Intelligent people with no compassion belong to the low-level.

4. Bottom-level people have neither compassion nor wisdom. They lack kindness and refuse to offer others any help. Moreover, they are not smart, having no wisdom at all. For example, they only want to enjoy the benefits of the organization they belong to without contributing anything in return. They not only refuse to give anything, but are also insatiably greedy. Being unreasonable, they encroach on others with their irrationality. Therefore, getting along with this type of person is truly difficult.

Compassion and wisdom are like our two hands. If we only have one hand, we cannot function well because we need the combination of both hands in order to work effectively. They are also like our two feet or the two wings of a bird. Humans walk with both feet, and birds need two wings to fly. Therefore, it is best to have both compassion and wisdom. If we lack either, it is like losing a hand or a foot, and it would be difficult for us to achieve success in anything we do.

Grading Ourselves

There are many types of people in society. Whether they are good or bad, kind or harmful, one could say there are still various "grades" within each type. For instance, top-grade people are capable and even-tempered. The second best are those who are capable but have a bad temper, the third grade are those who have a good temper but are incapable, and the worst are very bad-tempered without ability. In addition, there are four more categories to consider in grading ourselves.

1. First grade people emphasize trust and keep their promises. Reputation and trust are the intangible assets of people. "A promise is worth a thousand taels of gold" is a popular Chinese saying that emphasizes the weight and value of a promise. Some people are very serious about their reputation and keep to their promises very strictly. Sometimes, in order to protect their credibility, they will give all they have despite the difficulty in doing so. They are willing to sacrifice everything in order to keep a promise. People who adhere strictly to their trustworthiness and promises belong to the first grade.

2. Second grade people are open and candid. If people can be open, honest, and at ease in showing each other a kind, pure, and selfless heart, they are raising their character and their lives to a higher level. Therefore, people who are always open and candid with a selfless heart are true exemplars of cultivation and models of courage for us to emulate.

3. Third grade people are intelligent and articulate. Some people have glib tongues and are intelligent and capable. However, they lack restraint and integrity as they like to show off their keen awareness, their knowledge, and tal-

ents when they speak or work. They want to show people they are more capable, stronger, and better than those
around them. People like that may be intelligent and
articulate, but they are shallow and immature in conducting themselves. Therefore, they can only be classified as
the third grade.

4. Fourth grade people are selfish and self-absorbed. When
people only think of themselves, their achievements are
limited, but if they think of others, they can make broader connections. A key to conducting ourselves is being
mindful of others and their needs. People who only have
themselves on their minds all the time, leave no room for
the needs of others, and will inevitably mistreat others.
Selfish people are considered fourth grade because they
only care about themselves with no regard for others.

The biggest victory in life is not in defeating our enemies
but overcoming our own shortcomings. The glory of life does not
lie in being praised by our contemporaries but setting an example
for future generations. Therefore, the value of life depends on our
own efforts. As long as we have a sense of responsibility, we can
be considered capable. On the other hand, no matter how strong
our abilities may be, if we have no sense of responsibility, we will
only be considered mediocre. In grading ourselves, we need to
evaluate ourselves in order to see which grade we belong to.

People Are Like Horses

In Buddhist sutras, horses are often used as metaphors for people and their levels of cultivation. The natures of people and horses are similarly divided into four classes. First-class horses do not wait for the rider to raise the whip or holler. Once someone gets on, they will gallop away. Second class horses wait for a rider to wield a whip and bark commands before they start to gallop. A still lower class of horse will only move when whipped. For some horses, however, the more you whip them, the more they refuse to move, and simply lie down instead.

The different natures of people are like those of horses. Some people do not wait for others to show or teach them, for they know how to conduct themselves. There are people who are not clear on how to behave, but they will pick up right away after others give them a few suggestions. Some people are unhappy when anyone wants to direct them, and so they reject any advice. The worst type of person has to suffer first before learning how to act which is often too late. The following definitions explain how the different natures of people are like those of horses.

1. The wise will be aware once they see the whip. Top-grade horses will react on seeing the whip and begin to gallop right away. Similarly, the wise, when facing life and death and witnessing crimes and transgressions, can appreciate the meaning of impermanence. They will realize that they should be diligent in their cultivation.

2. The virtuous will only be aware when their hair is touched. For some horses, the whip must touch their hair before they react. Some people need to experience some heart-rending experience before they realize they should learn to be good and make progress in life. They can still be considered those who are mindful of cultivation.

3. The common will only be aware when their flesh is touched. For some horses, they must be whipped on the flesh and feel pain before they are willing to gallop. Such people will not shed tears unless they see a coffin. They wait until they are on their deathbeds to realize they have to cultivate themselves. They are, therefore, of the common lot.

4. The ignorant will only be aware when they are hurt to the bone. For some horses, they need to be whipped hard until they are in terrible pain before they know they have to start galloping. They are like many criminals who wait until they are shackled and put in jail before they have any remorse. They are truly ignorant.

People are like horses. There are good and bad horses as there are wise and ignorant people. The natures of horses reflect human characteristics. Are you holy, wise, common, or ignorant? We should all take a good look at ourselves.

Poverty and Wealth

Do you know how to evaluate people? How do you consider the good and bad, kindness and malice, honor and disgrace, wealth and poverty of people? How should you assess the level of people's cultivation and morals? Regardless of whether people are poor or wealthy, we can see from their speech and actions, such as giving and taking, where they stand. The following are some explanations for consideration:

1. Look at what poor people covet. Poverty can be a breeding ground for crime. Some people may have lived in poverty for too long and become fearful of it. Once they see a chance to make money, they may resort to any means available. They may think of all kinds of schemes over time to make money, and naturally they are unconcerned as to whether their actions are ethical or not. However, for people who have morals, their major concern is not about money, for they only fear of being without virtue. While they may not even have a place to live, they are still at ease and will not commit crimes to gain wealth. Therefore, when people have integrity in poverty, they have character and are truly wealthy.

2. Look at how poor people behave. As the saying goes, "One may be poor materially but not in spirit." Some people may be poor, but they do not degrade themselves, complain, or wallow in self-pity. They resolve to strive against all odds, and while they may have very little materially, their conduct is righteous and based on the correct view. What they do and how they act are in accordance with the motto, "See no impropriety, hear no impropriety, speak no impropriety, take no impropriety, and commit no impropriety." If people can remain ethi-

cal and uphold their character in poverty, they are wise and virtuous.

3. Look at what wealthy people give. Some people may be very rich. However, having a lot of money does not mean one is virtuous. Moreover, it does not signify that one is wise or possesses good human connections. We have to see how wealthy people use their money, and though some of them may make donations to others, we still have to look at how they do it. If they give with ulterior motives for the sake of making a good name for themselves or they donate only to their loved ones, the merit from their giving is limited. Knowing how to benefit country, society, and humanity with money is what a truly wise person will do.

4. Look at how people of high social status conduct themselves. People's honor or disgrace does not hinge on whether they are in high office or enjoy a high income. Rather, the focus is on whether or not their conduct radiates the brightness of human nature, and on whether or not they have integrity and compassion for all sentient beings. Some people may hold high office, but their conduct is so deplorable that they are lower than a panhandler on the street. On the other hand, there are people who are low in terms of social status but their morals and conduct are exemplary. They are the truly noble people.

Hence, people's poverty or wealth is not measured by how much money they have or how high their status may be. It all depends on their character and their conduct. If poor people have self-respect and resolve to improve themselves, they are not poor in spirit or morality. When people who enjoy high position or own immense wealth make use of their status and riches to serve the community and benefit humanity, they too are truly noble and wealthy.

Poor and Rich, Honored and Despised

In this world of such diverse morality, social status and position, there are the wise and the ignorant, the loyal and the treacherous, the rich and the poor, the humble and the arrogant, the generous and the selfish, as well as the sincere and the insincere. Why are there so many different kinds of people? Why is there a distinction too between rich and poor, honored and despised? Furthermore, according to the ancient philosopher Xunzi "Is it possible for one to be despised and then gain respectability, to be ignorant then wise, poor and then wealthy?" What follows is a discussion of how a person can change the condition of being poor and despised into being rich and honored.

1. The poor can become rich through hard work. People are poor because they do not have any money, and are thus often forced to drop out of school. However, as long as they have the willingness to work hard, have no fear of failure, and never give up hope or lose ambition, there will always be a chance for success and prosperity. "Poverty itself is not a terrible thing as long as it is not a self-imposed fate," said Benjamin Franklin. Both Andrew Carnegie of U.S. Steel and Konosuke Matsushita of Panasonic had humble beginnings. However, they tirelessly applied their minds and efforts to overcome their hardships in order to achieve incredible corporate success as well as unprecedented personal wealth. Therefore, it is possible for the poor to change their fortune through diligence and hard work.

2. The rich can gain honor through social position. Not every wealthy person in the world is satisfied with the money he or she has. Besides wealth, the rich may also want social status, power, and honor. They will seek

public office or a cabinet position in order to have social recognition. Once they have reached those goals, they will also gain the power and honor of a celebrity, allowing them to associate themselves with very important people and further elevate their own status. Therefore, the rich can be honored through social status and position.

3. The honored can become despised through selfishness. Some people are disliked regardless of their social prominence because they are selfish, stingy, corrupt, and ruthless. People fear them like a plague because of their illicit and violent activities. Therefore, the rich and the powerful can fail to gain popular support in their positions if they lack character, morality, and integrity. If they want to be truly honored for their fame and fortune, they must selflessly support their countries and be concerned about society's welfare. They have to be empathetic about the problems and sufferings of the people. If not, the honored too can become despised through selfishness.

4. The despised can regain respect through the Buddha. Some people are revered despite the fact that they are poor, lacking high status, uneducated, incapable, or even homeless. Why are they so well-respected when they could be easily looked down upon? It is because of their beliefs and their determination to never abandon their faith in the face of poverty. The teachings of their religion inspire them to remain unmoved by material gain and to be compassionate and kind. They can indeed regain respect if they are charitable and determined in their resolve to follow the right path. Therefore, a person who is despised can regain honor and respect through their faith in the Buddha.

A person's breadth of mind can determine his or her

wealth, and a person's cultivation can affect his or her respectability. In life, one's poverty, social position, wealth, and honor are neither permanent nor unchanging. The poor can acquire wealth and the despised honor, if they are willing to improve the necessary causes and conditions.

The Major Problems of Being Human

Laozi said, "The greatest problem for humanity is the physical body." Because of our bodies, we need to eat, sleep, and put on clothes. In addition, they must be cleansed, relieved, nourished, exercised, and kept healthy. We have to work incessantly to satisfy the body's many emotions, cravings, and needs. It is a lot of trouble indeed. But in reality, the major problems of being human are not confined to these obvious ones; the following are some of the hidden ones.

1. We can see fine details but not our own eyelashes. People can see the dust and sand in their environment, as well as other minute things, such as a hair or feather, but they cannot see their own eyelashes. This means we can easily notice the small faults of others, yet fail to see our own major shortcomings. What our eyes usually detect is how wrong or bad another person is, but we never reflect upon ourselves. Therefore, people can see others but not know themselves. Such is the shallowness of people.

2. We can lift a thousand pounds but not ourselves. A person's strength varies. Some who are not strong may be able to lift only five or ten pounds, while others can pick up twice as much. However, no matter how strong people are, it is impossible for them to lift themselves up. This means people have the strength to counter external circumstances, but often have no clue how to handle themselves. Being unable to be one's own master in life is sad indeed.

3. We can gain short-term benefit but remain unconcerned about long-term problems. Being greedy for short-term gains and lacking far-sightedness applies to the majority

of people. Often, we only care for benefits that are close at hand, and pay no attention to the potential danger down the line. As long as we profit and make money right away, we are happy and will pay almost no regard to the consequences. Therefore, corruption and bribery never cease in society, which can be explained by the saying: "Bodhisattvas fear causes; sentient beings fear effects." We have to bear in mind that "People who have no long-term plans will certainly face troubles close at hand." When we are only greedy for immediate gains and fail to appreciate problems in the future, we will soon find ourselves in major difficulty. Such is the ignorance of people.

4. We can view the whole world but not our own faults. We can travel the globe and view all the wonders of the world in Europe, the Americas, Asia, and Australia, taking in all the beautiful scenery. Moreover, we may be able to analyze the state of current events, the pros and cons, or the gains and losses of every issue, and be completely knowledgeable in every detail. However, we just cannot recognize our own faults. Such is the delusion of people.

In other words, the major problem of being human is failure to see our own mind, which in turn keeps us from knowing ourselves. As such, we will naturally not be able to learn, perfect, improve, or raise ourselves to higher levels. People should "not see the outside, but look inside; not look at others, but look at self." We should strive to rid ourselves of the problems described above.

The Most Fearful

We all have fears. People are afraid of the dark, suffering, pain, and death. Some people say war is most fearful, because bullets and bombs have no eyes and cannot see who they hit. Others say natural disasters are the worst, because floods, fire, and hurricanes are ruthless. In reality, what is most fearful is neither external violence nor outer circumstances. What we should fear most is ourselves. The reasons are as follows:

1. Poverty is not to be feared; lacking ability is. There is a common Chinese saying, "A dollar can crush a hero." Even heroes can lose their strength because of poverty. However, while a person may be poor financially, he or she should not be lacking in ambition. As long as we have capabilities, wisdom, and diligence, we will rise to the top and succeed one day. On the contrary, the worst fear is when we are lazy, lacking ability and skill. In that case, even if we are very wealthy, there will be a day when all our money will be used up. Therefore, poverty is not to be feared, but lacking ability is.

2. A lowly position is not to be feared; lacking ambition is. The sutras state, "All sentient beings have Buddha Nature." Since we all have Buddha Nature, there should not be any distinction over social class. However, it is human nature to categorize people into different levels based on their backgrounds, professions, income, and academic achievements. In ancient India during the Buddha's time, there were four castes. Among the Buddha's disciples, Nidhi and Upala came from the slave caste, the most inferior of the four. However, they did not lose their ambition or blame themselves for their low social position. After they followed the Buddha and

became monks, they were very diligent in their cultivation and attained enlightenment. They were illustrations of the saying: "Heroes have no fear of being born low, because throughout history generals and ministers have not come from one breed." If we have ambition, we will have the strength to break through difficulties. If on the other hand, we have no resolve, we will not accomplish anything. Therefore, being in a low position is not to be feared, but lacking ambition is.

3. Fatigue is not to be feared; lacking willpower is. Our physical strength is limited, and we get tired after working long hours. Therefore, we need appropriate rest because doing so is essential to moving ahead on the path. We should not fear being tired for the moment, but we should be wary of losing our willpower in face of setbacks in whatever we do. When we are tired, run out of steam, and lose the perseverance to progress, we may fall down and become unable to recover from our failure. "There is no worse grief than a dead heart." The loss of our self-confidence or our focus on things is a very serious crisis. On the other hand, when we have resolve, we will have the strength to move on. So when we have willpower and perseverance, being tired is not to be feared.

4. Chaos is not to be feared; lacking poise is. The best time to test our focus and cultivation is when we face sudden changes. While some people can easily become nervous and confused in dealing with a crisis, others are able to remain calm and unperturbed, even in matters of life and death. In Chinese history, renowned strategists, such as Xie An of the Eastern Jin Dynasty and Zhuge Liang of the Three Kingdoms Period, were known to remain cool whenever they faced a massive army of enemy troops. They were able to take command of the situation without losing their focus. Their poise is hard for the average

person to match today. However, feeling nervous and confused in the face of emergency is not a problem, as long as we also have the strength to calm ourselves down. We must have poise so that we will not make fools of ourselves, because if we lack concentration and cultivation, we will become the laughingstock of others.

We need not be the most courageous in the world, but we should never be a coward defeated by our own hands. We should, therefore, bear in mind what is most fearful in life—ourselves.

The Imperfections of Life

Beauty in life comes from its imperfections. People need not necessarily be perfect because their imperfections are also beautiful. Likewise, imperfections are the essence and reality of life. We should, therefore, understand, appreciate and even exploit life's "imperfections," altering them when necessary. However, we must not allow them to become our regret. The following are ways to understand the imperfections of life.

1. Being poor is not in itself shameful, but lacking resolve is. The ancients "derided prostitution and not poverty," while people today do the opposite. The truth is that there is nothing to be ashamed of in being poor, because real shame lies in the lack of resolve to improve our conditions. As humans, we should never be poor in our resolve. We may suffer temporary setbacks, but we should not be concerned about our financial gains or losses. As long as we have the resolve and vow to succeed, we need not fear the lack of achievements.

2. Being inferior is not in itself despicable, but being incapable is. It is human nature to scorn poverty and inferiority and value wealth and nobility. However, true inferiority is not being without status and riches. There is a saying, "Lacking status is not inferior; being shameless is." People who are shameless are inevitably impoverished and despised. Those unwilling to improve their morals and wisdom will end up with lowly character. There are people who are lazy, unwilling to do any meaningful work, who loaf around all day instead, making no progress in life. The abuse and waste of their own potential is the most despicable.

3. Being old is not in itself regrettable, but being unaccom-

plished is. Growing old is not a question of age but rather a state of mind. What we should fear is the degeneration of our spirit and mental strength, not the increasing number of years. We usually feel sad that we are getting old, not having too many days left in life. The reality is that it is not important how long our life is. It is how much merit and achievement we leave behind in the world that counts. Have we lived the true meaning of life? Zheng Cheng'gong, the historic figure who contributed the most to Taiwan, only lived for thirty-eight years; the renowned Song General Yue Fei, who served his country with utmost loyalty, only lived thirty-nine years; Jesus, thirty-six years; Yan Hui, the premier disciple of Confucius, thirty-five years; the Buddhist monastic Sengzhao, author of *The Commentary of Master Sengzhao* [*Zhao Lun*], thirty-two years; and Alexander the Great, thirty-three years. However, their morals, character, merits, and achievements are still considered exemplary and revered even in today's world. Therefore, we should not be saddened by aging, because it is more important for us to live a meaningful life.

4. Death in itself is not to be mourned, but dying without any merit is. Where there is birth or life, there is death. The latter is not necessarily sorrowful. If we are able to bequeath our legacy in terms of our words, our moral conduct, and our achievements, we are leaving behind eternal life in the world, so it does not really matter how long we live. It is, therefore, imperative for us to leave something behind through our moral conduct and career for the benefit of others, as well as a few words of wisdom for them to remember.

Seeking a life of happiness and perfection is the inherent desire of human beings. However, in the course of perfecting life, we should cultivate a tolerant heart for the imperfections in life.

To Obey and Follow

To obey and follow orders are the duties of soldiers. It is said, "Dealing with the reasonable is training; dealing with the unreasonable is tempering." When we can accept something unreasonable, we will definitely not reject the reasonable. The truth is that to obey and follow are the ways to establish social order and demonstrate moral conduct. Nowadays, people are not keen on following orders and often rebel against authority, leading to disorder and immorality. In order to establish a society that is ethical and orderly, we should learn to obey and follow. There are four levels of obeying and following for different kinds of people.

1. Ordinary people obey out of fear. It is commonly accepted that subordinates should obey their superiors, students their teachers, and children their parents. However, some people have very strong egos and only their own views matter. Even their superiors, with reason and authority, may not be able to win their wholehearted acceptance. Such opinionated people will just pretend to obey while discrediting others at the same time. The only alternative is to subdue them by threatening a loss of their benefits. When they only submit out of a fear of losing something, rather than having true appreciation, they can only be considered base and common.

2. Benevolent people obey out of devotion. There is a saying about human relationships, "Some love will exist in seeing each other again." When we treat people well, supporting and protecting them in ordinary times, they will repay us with respect and deference. They will also be willing to make sacrifices for us out of gratitude. People who value morality and are grateful for what they

receive are indeed benevolent.

3. Virtuous people obey out of compassion. Some people are righteous, do not seek fame or fortune, live a simple life, and have little craving. They enjoy practicing charity and are generous, for they are happy to contribute toward any benevolent cause or share what they have with others. They can be considered virtuous. As they naturally follow what is compassionate, they will certainly abide by what is necessary to achieve a goal.

4. Wise people obey out of respect for the truth. Some people do not necessarily submit for money, love, or power. However, they will absolutely comply with the truth. "Having reverence for the law brings joy every day; taking advantage of the truth produces worries daily." If people really obey the truth and have faith in it, they will certainly have an open heart and a smooth path in life because they have wisdom.

There are different levels of abidance. When people comply out of fear, they are still corrigible. If they do it out of gratitude, they can succeed in life, and those who adhere to social welfare out of compassion will achieve even greater rewards. Most importantly, people must abide by the truth, because those who submit to the truth are certainly wise.

Good Causes and Conditions

People may not need to believe in the Dharma, but they cannot afford not to believe in the Law of Cause and Effect. This law is not a matter of opinion, but is rather the truth of life and the rule for conducting all actions. We reap good fruit when we sow a good seed and a bad one when conditions are adverse and/or the seed is poor, for we are our own gardener. If we want to live with fortune, fulfillment, and joy, we have to cultivate good causes and conditions. The following four points are the key to creating good causes and conditions.

1. Avoid breaking promises and trust. In life, trust should come first for us. "A promise is worth a thousand taels of gold." When others ask us for help, if we are able, we should agree to assist them, and if not, we should explain the reason why we cannot, rather than make a promise lightheartedly and forget about it later. When we fail to keep a promise more than a few times, people will be disappointed with us or even bear a grudge against us. They may decide not to have anything to do with us anymore, and then it will be too late for us to make it up to them. Therefore, we must be trustworthy. We need to be on time in keeping appointments, and never break any promise we make with others. Trust is an important condition in establishing ourselves in life. We can never afford to ignore it.

2. Guard strictly against being talkative and argumentative. "When someone slanders us, rather than argue, we should be tolerant." Since there is no urgency to defend ourselves when slandered, there is even less of a reason to argue with others in ordinary times. However, some people enjoy winning a debate and arguing with others.

Once they open their mouths, they cannot stop and simply carry on endlessly. They do not realize that people will retreat quickly on meeting someone who is quarrelsome. The reason is that although argumentative people may sound reasonable on the surface, they tend to exaggerate in their reasoning, and over time others will see through them. Naturally, people would also want to stay clear of them. Therefore, if we do not want to be a person that people avoid, we should guard strictly against being overly talkative and argumentative.

3. Treat others with generosity and openness. When we have a big and open heart and treat others with magnanimity, there are clear pathways everywhere we go. If we have a narrow mind and are mean-spirited to people, there will be thorny bushes at every turn. In being generous, we gain people's friendship. If on the other hand, we are merciless, mean, and unforgiving when we are right, we will make enemies easily. Because when we forgive others, we are actually freeing ourselves. There is a saying, "Those who enjoy good fortune are inevitably forgiving, and being magnanimous, they gain an even better fortune." For those who are generous and forgiving, they can develop deep resources, make broad connections with people, and are able to gain much support in their career. So it is important to be generous in order to succeed.

4. Emphasize basic etiquette and courtesy. In dealing with others, we should never think that courtesy is no longer important because we know each other so well. Actually, courtesy is something in accord with reason and ethics. *The Three-Character Classic* [*San Zi Jing*] states, "[Let there be] righteousness between ruler and minister; closeness between father and son; and harmony between husband and wife." In the family, there should be respect between spouses and courtesy between parents and chil-

dren. Moreover, the righteousness between a ruler and his ministers should never be compromised. In our daily life, friends, neighbors, or coworkers should greet each other with "how are you" or "good morning," a smile, a nod, or joined palms. This is just basic etiquette between people in showing others respect. It is a basic exchange of goodwill in human relationships that should never be missing in life.

In treasuring our fortune, we should cherish our present situation; in making broad connections with others, we are enriching our future. When we are faced with setbacks and difficulties, as long as we are willing to change our causes and create good conditions in human relationships, we will be able to realize a wonderful future.

Knowing Ourselves

There are many people in the world. Each of them has a unique personality, as well as likes and dislikes. Moreover, each person has his or her own thinking, views, ideas, abilities, skills, and experience. What is most important is that people come to know themselves, no matter what their strengths, weaknesses, or characteristics may be. When we know ourselves, we know how to handle our shortcomings and bring our talents into full play. The following are some guidelines for knowing ourselves.

1. The worst problem in life is not knowing our faults. Not knowing our own mistakes and shortcomings is the worst problem in life. We cannot be perfect, for we all have certain faults and inadequacies. According to a Buddhist saying, "People are not perfect sages; they cannot be without faults. Knowing one's faults and correcting them is the greatest virtue." In addition, we need the courage to face our shortcomings and rectify them so that we can continue to improve and become someone more useful. If on the other hand, we fail to appreciate our mistakes and try to cover them, or we lack the courage to face them, then we will never have the opportunity to correct them. Naturally, we will never improve and make progress. Therefore, not knowing our faults is the worst problem in life.

2. The most beautiful virtue in life is correcting our mistakes. Zilu, a disciple of Confucius, was overjoyed in learning about his mistakes; Yu the Great bowed in gratitude when learning about his faults. Over the ages, the virtuous sages were always pleased to hear others point out their shortcomings. They were more than happy to accept the advice others gave them. Therefore, we

should "not be afraid to correct our mistakes." When we are happy to hear about our faults, we will improve and be able to succeed. However, some people tend to protect and cover up their mistakes. When others point them out, they feel hurt and upset. How can anyone who does not want to correct his or her mistakes improve and progress? Therefore, the greatest virtue in life is being able to make amends after realizing one's own faults.

3. The most precious quality in life is having good reasoning and upholding righteousness. Having power and influence is not what is most precious in the world. "It is difficult under common circumstances for people to uphold righteousness even after learning about it; it is the habit of the virtuous sages to follow righteousness just by seeing it." As long as people can reason well and think clearly, they will find it easy to conduct any matter. When people are active in upholding righteousness, they will certainly win the respect of others. Therefore, when we can reason well and uphold righteousness, we are halfway to success in life.

4. The most disgraceful flaw in life is being corrupt and having no sense of shame. "A tree without bark bears no fruit; a person without a sense of shame finds it very difficult to enter the Way." If a person is corrupt, impure, unscrupulous, and shameless, and yet is unwilling to change from past mistakes or practice benevolence, such a person can never succeed in anything, for he or she will end up being despised by others. Therefore, if we want to succeed in life, we must strive and work hard. When we realize that, in order for us to strive and improve, we first need to appreciate shame and humility, we can then truly succeed in life.

In getting along with people, not knowing our faults is very dangerous, and being ignorant of our strengths is regrettable. If we fail to appreciate what is problematic, beautiful, valuable, and ignoble in life, we will find that society will not accept us.

Prescription for Calming Minds

When people live in prosperity, it is easy for them to remain calm and peaceful. However, once they face adversity, it may be difficult for them to stay composed. Remaining calm and composed is essential for dealing with emergencies and difficulties. When the commanding general remains calm while directing a battle from the front lines, his thinking will be sensible and clear, and as a result, he will give effective orders. In the business world, if entrepreneurs can remain calm in the face of gains and losses, they will be able to prosper. If students can stay composed for examinations and tests, they will get good grades. When the police stay calm enforcing law, they will win the respect of the people. Therefore, remaining calm and peaceful is the greatest cultivation in conducting ourselves and dealing with situations. The following are some guidelines for how to maintain calmness for self and others in order to maintain harmony:

1. Remain impartial in dealing with the conflicts of others. People often start fighting and arguing with their friends, relatives, neighbors, and family members over different views or small gain with neither party willing to back off or give in. If we are caught in the middle of such a fight, what should we do? The best thing to do is to be fair and just without being partial to either side, so as to avoid upsetting others and incurring any hate or anger.

2. Maintain a kind heart when facing impulsive and violent people. We often come across friends or associates who are very impulsive and violent at work or in the community. What should we do in the face of such vicious and unkind people? We should not bicker and fight with them in a similar manner but rather use compassion. We should try to understand the root of their negative emo-

tions and violent acts and not respond in kind. When we maintain a very calm and kind mind, we can resolve any problem.

3. Do not push our advice when others are attached to their views and refuse to listen. Sometimes we may encounter a debate or argument with both parties remaining adamant in their views and unwilling to reach a consensus. At this point, we should not push our advice or try to mediate for them, hoping they can reach an agreement. Because they have become so hotheaded, they would not be able to listen even to the best advice and reasoning. So if we want to counsel them, we should wait until they have cooled down before we try to reason with them tactfully in private. In this way, we might be more effective in resolving the situation.

4. Keep silent when the right and wrong between people is unclear. When there are conflicts and arguments, it is best to keep silent before we can actually figure out the sequence of events and see who is right or wrong. After we learn about the situation and the development of the matter, we can proceed to mediate and assist, and thereby avoid making matters worse.

We should not fight and get angry, because that will not solve any problem. Remaining calm and peaceful instead develops our wisdom, and with wisdom, we can find the solution.

To Be Honest and Righteous

In conducting ourselves, we need to be honest and considerate so that others will inevitably be drawn to us. We will become like high mountains that birds and animals flock to naturally. We should never be harsh and mean to others. The following are a few keys on how to be honest and considerate.

1. Do not blame others for small mistakes. This is a virtue of cultivation. Some people never offer even a word of praise to others no matter how good the accomplishment. However, when others make a small mistake, they are harsh in their criticism. Such people lack compassion and morality. Therefore, in conducting ourselves, we should be tolerant and counsel others when they make small mistakes, because it is a form of cultivation and a virtue in treating others with kindness.

2. Do not expose others' secrets. We increase our own merit when we refrain from publicizing the secrets of others. There are people who never mention the virtuous deeds others do, no matter how exceptional and outstanding they may be. However, once they learn of a small personal matter of another, they will blow it all out of proportion, even to the point of spreading rumors about. Their behavior attests to the saying, "Good deeds never leave home; bad deeds spread for a thousand miles." When we publicize the secrets of others, we expose our own poor ethical standards, and at the same time, we make more enemies. Therefore, we have to be considerate in conducting ourselves. Merit will always come to those who are considerate.

3. Do not bear any grudges. This is the cultivation of our morals. Some people will easily forget all the kindness

others have ever shown them, but they will remember very clearly all the transgressions committed against them, for such people are very small-minded. The truth is that no matter how close friends or family members may be, we will sooner or later hurt one another unintentionally. If we are petty and will not let go of even an insignificant comment someone has made about us or a disappointment we suffered from that person, we will be left with few intimate relatives or friends. We should instead think positively in every matter because that is the balm for human relationships, as well as the foundation for cultivating our ethics.

4. Do not focus on the gains and losses of others. This is the way of cultivating tolerance and morals. We need to be magnanimous in order to win people's hearts. Tolerance should be our teacher in life so that we can cultivate magnanimity. In handling matters and making friends, we sometimes make some gain because of our friends' support; and at other times, because of our friends, we may suffer some loss. By not taking every gain and loss to heart, we can better expand our capacity for tolerance, and improve our morality and merit.

Treating others with honesty and consideration is a virtue that wins their love and respect. When we lack morality and are harsh or mean in dealing with others, we will only gain their contempt. People who are honest and considerate will gain depth and breadth in their cultivation, make broad connections with people, and win more support in their careers. To be honest and considerate is therefore the way to succeed.

Wise and Courageous People

Heroes who are both wise and courageous have been admired and praised throughout history. How can we become wise and courageous? The following are some guidelines:

1. The wise comprehend all through knowledge and wisdom. The catalyst for civilization progressing so quickly is not material wealth, rather, it stems from the culmination of people's wisdom. Wisdom is wealth. The physical strength of an individual is limited, while true potential lies in our innate wisdom. The wise can understand every matter through their knowledge and wisdom. There are so many different professional fields all requiring profound expertise. But regardless of whether people are scholars or professors of science, physics, chemistry, medicine, or literature, they all rely on one thing—wisdom! With wisdom, they know how to apply their knowledge to comprehend the universe and life. Therefore, the wise are never tired of learning, because they use knowledge and wisdom to comprehend everything.

2. The benevolent tolerate all with love. People are not necessarily wise, and not everyone can become a scholar or an expert. However, at the very least, we can be a benevolent person. To be benevolent is to embrace all people and matters with love and compassion. We should be able to tolerate our family, friends, relatives, and the organization or company we belong to and work for. We should not only be able to accept our loved ones and people we care for, but also tolerate those we do not like. Being able to tolerate the shortcomings of others is the greatest strength of a benevolent person.

3. The courageous sacrifice all they have with righteousness. Who is courageous is not determined by who has a larger fist or who can display more bravado in a fight with knives or guns. The truly courageous focus on righteousness, for they take both righteousness and love very seriously. If given a small benefit by another, they will repay that person ten or even a hundredfold. They are even willing to sacrifice their lives to do so.

4. The loyal contribute all they possess with sincerity. Over the ages, loyal ministers or servants have served their ruler or master with sincerity. They were devoted, loyal, dutiful, honest, and unwavering in their heart. They were also willing to sacrifice everything for their leader or commit a lifetime of service to their master. Therefore, the loyal contribute everything with sincerity, while people who treat others with sincerity are loyal.

As Buddhists, we should practice both wisdom and compassion. In conducting ourselves, we need to be both loyal and courageous. Wisdom without compassion is wayward intuition, and compassion straying from wisdom is worldly love. It is only the bodhisattva spirit of "compassion for all" that can inspire a wise person to understand, a benevolent person to love, and a courageous person to apply himself or herself. By supporting one another, we can benefit all sentient beings.

The Ability to Know People

The ability to know people and how to use their skills is the basic quality a leader should possess, because people all have their different talents, abilities, skills, personalities, likes, and dislikes. We should make use of people's strengths. However, if we do not know them, we will not know how to work with them, and if we cannot work with them, we should not become a leader. The following are keys to knowing people:

1. We need to know people's abilities. People have different abilities. Some may be good at physical tasks, while others are more adept at mental ones. We should give them room to bring their capabilities into full play. If we do not allow a capable person to give his or her best, it is like putting a skilled basketball player on the bench instead of letting him or her play. It is like a prized racehorse whose capacity is not recognized. It will "end up suffering at the hands of slave drivers and die working in the stables, never to be known as that horse of exceptional speed."

2. We need to know people's special talents. When given favorable conditions, people exhibit their talents while working. In the past, many heroic figures bemoaned how their talents went unrecognized. It is of course a personal misfortune if one's talents are not given the opportunity to flower, and it is even a loss for the organization to which they belong. Therefore, we must give those with talent the best chance, and not try to suppress them. If we do not delegate authority to them so they can make their own decisions, they will only feel useless and overlooked even if they are extremely learned and multi-talented.

3. We need to know people's ability to connect. Sometimes, a person may be limited in ability and not really talented in any special way. However, he or she relates well to people and makes very broad connections. Knowing how to make use of one's ability to connect with others is also very important. Therefore, a supervisor who knows how to work well with people should focus on both abilities and human connections and conditions.

4. We need to know people's integrity. Some intelligent and capable people may be unethical. On the other hand, while others may fall short in skill, they are still righteous. If we can make use of their integrity, they will be of great value. In the past, some loyal servants followed their masters for decades. The reason for that was integrity. By the same token, people in the past delegated authority to their housekeeper who was capable of managing the family's properties and all its human relationships very well. Therefore, it is important for us to make good use of people with integrity.

As the saying goes, "Knowing one's own situation and that of the enemy guarantees victory in every battle." Being a supervisor or even just one in the crowd, besides having the ability to know ourselves, we should also know people.

How to Evaluate People

Evaluation is a very important process for any modern country or society. For instance, schools are evaluated regularly by the Ministry of Education to ensure the quality of education, just as factories are regulated by the Ministry of Economic Affairs for quality control. Religious establishments are evaluated by the Ministry of Interior for their social and educational functions. Similarly, people have to be evaluated in some way or another to determine their value and abilities. Here are four points to consider in evaluating a person.

1. Only in the long run, will an individual's true colors be revealed. A horse's strength is tested when the road is long. A good thoroughbred is different from a nag in its ability to travel "a thousand miles a day." In determining the strength of a person's legs, we need not look any further than how far one has walked. Therefore, it is only after a series of tests and evaluations that we are able to judge a person's real strength in handling different kinds of responsibilities.

2. Only when a boat has capsized, will an experienced swimmer be spotted. Under everyday circumstances, it is not easy for someone to fully display his or her swimming skills or knowledge of the water. However, if a boat capsizes one day, a person's skill as an experienced swimmer would immediately become known. Similarly, a person's potential will remain dormant until tested in an emergency, and his or her maturity and steadiness will become clear only through his or her reaction to the given situation.

3. Only when power and influence are lost, will true friendship be realized. In a relationship, adversity will reveal

a person's true heart and intention. When we are with means, it is easy to be surrounded every day by fickle friends who will not hesitate to leave us at the first sign of trouble. They will not be there for us in times of need, and will be quick to abandon us when we have become impoverished. It is in times of poverty and failure that we really discover who our true friends are. "Friendship that is present regardless of the highs and lows" is sincere and genuine, and reflects the true reality of human nature.

4. Only when there is poverty, will honor and integrity be understood. It is often the case that when we run into bad times, adversity and trouble will arrive together without a break. For example, a person might become unemployed or bankrupt, and still have to confront creditors who come calling daily. However, if such a person still upholds the rules of morality, acts compassionately and responsibly without complaining and blaming others, what can we say about his or her character and integrity in times of hardship and helplessness? Undoubtedly, we would consider such a person as someone who can withstand every kind of test.

In this world, everything is impermanent and people and things keep changing. Since everybody is constantly changing, we cannot evaluate a person based on just one moment or from just one side. Therefore, there is a saying, "when all prosperity is exhausted and lost, we can see one's true value."

Knowing People

According to the saying, "We know a person's face but not his or her heart." Getting to know people is actually not difficult. As long as we observe them well, there is no one in the world whom we cannot understand. The following are four methods for doing so:

1. We know people are wise when they are not deluded in dealing with matters. In the Chinese language, the character "wisdom" is made up of two characters: "day" and "know." Over time, if we can learn, listen well, and see broadly, we will become more knowledgeable and not be confused, and naturally we will gain "wisdom." If we want to see whether or not people have wisdom, we have to observe how they deal with day-to-day matters. When they are not tentative, and have no doubts in giving very clear instructions for every matter that needs attention, it is clear that they are wise. In reality, people are confused only because of selfishness. Without selfishness, everything is clear, and wisdom naturally arises.

2. We know people are righteous when they do not shirk difficulties. Difficulties are the first steps toward the truth. If people are brave in taking up responsibility, facing problems without shunning their duty, never claiming undue credit or taking on easy jobs while passing on the hard parts to others, they are the righteous ones. They make good friends because they have the courage to take up any challenge no matter how difficult the job. They are ethical and virtuous. In making friends with people like that, we will gain a lot.

3. We know people are honest when they act scrupulously with money. Keeping up appearances is not as important

as honesty and integrity. If we do not forget the virtues of honesty and humility, we will establish ourselves well in life without corruption. In business partnerships, some people will forget about righteousness if tempted by profit, and think of various means to get more than their fair share. On the other hand, there are those who not only refuse to accept illicit gains, but also are eager to donate what they rightfully receive. They are the honest officials in public positions, and as ordinary citizens, they have self-respect since they choose to live simple and honest lives. This brings to mind the saying, "Frugality cultivates honesty, and honesty gives rise to a clear mind." If we are honest in conducting ourselves, our minds will be like a clear mirror for all to see.

4. We know people are upright when they are not confused in facing situations. We must be upright in conducting ourselves. "Winning a reputation is not as good as having right intentions." Therefore, we need to correct ourselves first before we can improve what happens around us. How do we assess if people are upright? We can see this virtue in an emergency when everyone is panicking. If a person is not confused and upset, we can see how his or her mind is so open, peaceful, and at ease as he or her can remain calm. People who are upright naturally stand tall and walk straight. Their character is like a tree growing straight, whose shadow will naturally be straight as well.

In getting along with others, we have to see clearly what kind of person they are and know them well. More importantly, we also need self-reflection. Being able to see, understand, and know ourselves clearly is even more important than knowing other people.

Being Inspired

People are sentient beings because they have emotions. They can be deeply moved to tears by a person, a few words, a certain situation, a good book or movie. Being inspired is a display of emotions, and this is what connects humans to each other. The world of inspiration is very beautiful and enriches our life. A person who is easily moved usually lives a more meaningful life, because in being moved, he or she manifests the Buddha mind and Buddha Nature. Being inspired can be understood as follows:

1. Being inspired by the high harmonizing with the low. Within an organization, if the supervisors are moved by the hard work of their subordinates and the latter are touched by the support of the former, there will be harmony. In the family, parents should always think of ways to inspire their children, and vice versa. Thus, there will be respect and love for each other as they get along with joy in harmony.

2. Being inspired by the love and friendship between people. In interacting with one another, being inspired is an important element. We should feel affected by the things we say to each other and what we do for each other in our everyday life. In addition, we should feel touched by the courtesy and humility we show one another. As such, regardless of whether it is with friends, coworkers, or neighbors, we will be able to establish very good friendships. Therefore, we need to be inspired by and rejoice in what others do in daily life. Likewise, what we do ourselves should also be able to inspire others.

3. Being inspired by an exchange between minds. In Buddhism, there is the ideal of "mind linking with mind." Regardless of whether the source of our inspira-

tion is from people or from the Buddha, when we are moved, we will be able to communicate. When Sakyamuni Buddha first had the resolve to liberate all sentient beings and started cultivating in his previous lives, he cut his own flesh to feed an eagle and gave up his life as food for a tigress, all because he was moved to do so. By the same token, the major disciples of the Buddha were inspired to follow him and propagate the Dharma. Avalokitesvara Bodhisattva has inspired and supported us because he was moved by our suffering. Being moved is the exchange between hearts and minds, for when we are moved, we will become inspired.

4. Being inspired by the cultivation between self and others. Among the different methods of cultivation, "being inspired" is a very important one. For instance, we may be moved upon seeing the image of the Buddha, observing others chanting and bowing with devotion, noticing the generosity of others in giving. Furthermore, witnessing the suffering of sentient beings, we may be so moved as to ignite the resolve and compassion to help them.

Therefore, whether or not a person has the Dharma within him, we just need to see if he can be inspired. In our cultivation, if we can cultivate the capacity to be moved, it is easier for us to gain achievement. Therefore, we should be mindful of how we can inspire others with our speech and action. Having compassion, resolve, humility, patience, and diligence in conducting ourselves, is the best cultivation.

Cherish Our Fortune

We all wish for good fortune. In the Chinese tradition, each household posts calligraphy of the characters "spring" and "fortune" at New Year's time, signifying "As spring arrives in the world, good fortune fills the house." During ordinary times, people wish for the "arrival of the Five Fortunes," and friends often bless each other with wishes of good fortune. Fortune means happiness and good luck. Buddhism also talks about fortune and merit and is much more thorough in its interpretation. Good fortune is not, however, something in the hands of deities. We need to cultivate it. Besides enjoying our fortune, we also have to cherish what we have. The following are ways to cherish our fortune:

1. Cherish time in our daily activities. The world is "half and half": half of it is day, and the other half night. The famed Chinese poet Tang Bohu wrote in his "Seventy Poem," "The first ten years I was too young, and the last ten too old. / There were only fifty in the middle, half of which passed away in the night." In our limited time, the ancients admonished us with: "The day has passed, and our life, is thus reduced." They reminded us to cherish time as we would our life. If we have all the wealth in the world but not the time and good health to enjoy and use it, we would realize the vanity of it all. Therefore, we must treasure time because time is life, for in wasting time, we are killing life. When we are punctual for an appointment, we are treasuring our own time and that of others. When we say we need to save, it should not just be about money, because time is just as important.

2. Cherish resources in our daily use. We should not casually destroy anything we use in our daily life such as a chair, a table, a cup, a plate, or even a thread and needle.

We must not lightly discard a piece of vegetable because there is useful life in all things. By randomly destroying things, we are reducing their life span and their use. It is a form of killing to waste our fortune. Therefore, we need to cherish resources in our daily use.

3. Cherish our words when speaking. *The Analects of Confucius* state, "A single statement can bring prosperity to a nation; a single statement can bring disaster to a nation." If something is well-spoken, it can bring others joy like a lotus blossoming from the tongue. If something is not said properly, it kills others' hope like swords and knives. The renowned Chinese strategist, Sunzi, once said, "Offering others helpful words is as precious as gold. Hurting others with cruel speech is as vicious as sharp knives." Buddhism also advocates, "Sealing our mouth and hiding our tongue, is the first step in cultivation." We make mistakes if we talk too much, for "troubles come from the mouth." Therefore, we have to be careful with every word we speak. To be ethical with our speech is an important cultivation in life.

4. Cherish our connections with people. As the saying goes, "We meet because we have a karmic connection." Even if we meet our family, friends, coworkers, or strangers only once, we should cherish our connection with them in the here and now. We should offer them a kind word, smile, and assistance. Appreciating every small connection and condition we have with people is the wonderful recipe for dealing with the world.

Our fortune and merit are like deposits in the bank. We should cherish what we have and not use them recklessly or keep using them without making further deposits. Otherwise, the day will come when all is gone. We will gain fortune and merit only if we cherish and cultivate them.

Keys to Living Well

We all need to live, but not everybody knows how to live well. Life is not just about clothes, food, shelter, and transportation, nor is it just eating, drinking, and having fun. We should have a mission and objectives in life to accomplish. Even though we may all know how to live, because our attitudes towards life are all different, the quality and meaning of life will naturally vary from person to person. For instance, some people live artistically, carefree, and with substance, while others live with worry and frustration, finding it hard to settle down. How do we live a healthy life? The following four points are keys to living well:

1. Eat three proper meals a day. "Food is supreme for people." People rely on food and drink to nourish their physical bodies in order to survive. However, if we do not eat properly, we might get sick. For instance, some people eat too much rich food and become overweight. Not only will being overweight make it difficult for them to move about, it is unhealthy as well. If we want good health, we must eat properly. We should eat at the right time and only the appropriate amount. We should consider food as medicine. Following the "Five Contemplations for Eating," would be the best way to keep us in good health.

2. Dress appropriately for the occasion. There is a popular saying, "The statues of the Buddha need to be embellished with gold; people need to be dressed in clothing." Besides food, clothes are a major part of life. They keep us warm and enhance our looks. We should wear the proper attire when we go out according to social convention. How and what we put on for any occasion reflect our status and cultivation. Therefore, we should

dress with respect to our age, status, and the occasion. This is the key to clothing. We need not pursue the latest fashion or be glamorous. Neither should we be fanciful or unconventional by putting on strange couture to attract others' attention.

3. Work and rest accordingly. We only have twenty-four hours in a day, and though we all have different jobs, we still need to maintain a normal schedule for sleep, work, exercise, and rest. By working and resting accordingly, we benefit our health, build our character, and enhance our work, and our social and family life. Therefore, we should never invert day and night in our schedule, because our daily living will be in chaos, and our life at some point will collapse.

4. Cultivate a calm spiritual life. While we need a material life, we also need a spiritual one. When our spiritual life is well-organized, our body and mind will be in balance and our emotions stable. By engaging in a spiritual practice, we can elevate our life. In addition to working each day, we need to find time to be alone so that our spirit can have a moment of rest. We should talk to ourselves, reflecting on the day's occurrences. Furthermore, we can recharge our spirit through religious practices such as bowing, chanting, and meditating. Furthermore, reading, hobbies, recreation, and art are also means to nourish our mind so we are prepared to face a new day.

We all have to make our own arrangements and plan our own daily lives in order for life to have variety. Even though we may choose to live simply, we still need to look after our daily activities well. We should never live in chaos without any positive note in life.

The Way to Cultivate

Learning the Dharma is not just something we talk about. It is a way of thinking, belief, and cultivation. Cultivation is not the suffering, joy, glory, and failure that we see externally, rather, it is developing a realistic appreciation and practice through which the brightness of our inner nature can shine forth. It is the revelation of the strength of our compassion and resolve as we remain steadfast in our practice. There are many ways to cultivate. The following are a few guidelines for consideration:

1. Praise others often for their kind acts. Speech is an important tool in human communication. If used inappropriately, it can be used as a weapon to harm others. Therefore, we need to learn to speak positively. Giving others praise according to circumstances, it is also a form of cultivation. For instance, we can praise others for their kind deeds or commend them for their benevolent character. In Buddhism, taking joy in others' good deeds is a method of practice. It allows us to practice praising others in accordance with the situation. This is the first thing we should do in treating others well while at the same time practicing cultivation ourselves.

2. Counsel others when they are in trouble. Practicing the Dharma does not necessarily mean going to the mountains to practice or just donating money. Sometimes, a few kind words, a kind deed, or a smile can create many positive conditions for us in life and accrue more merit. For example, when we see others who are deluded or lost and not thinking clearly, we need to remind them of the possibilities they have and guide them out of their trouble with encouragement. We cannot give up on them and reject them because they have problems. In practicing

the Dharma, we must have the compassion to not give up on any single sentient being. Therefore, counseling others when they are in trouble is the second most important cultivation for self and others.

3. Work harder when others praise us. Gain, loss, defamation, glory, praise, ridicule, sorrow, and joy are called the "Eight Winds" in Buddhism. They are the eight kinds of states that influence our minds. We need to reflect upon ourselves when others criticize us. Even if others praise us, we should be humble and review whether we are worth it. We should be not only grateful but also more aware of our own inadequacies and inabilities. Only by always striving to progress, will we deserve praise.

4. Be aware when others slander us. According to the saying, "When praise arrives, slander will follow." There is no one standard for good and bad in this world. There were many historic heroes who were idolized by some people and yet vilified by others. Even an ordinary person will be praised and admired as well as criticized and attacked. Therefore, we should not get angry when we are slandered. We should take the criticism and slander as a warning for our own cultivation, for these are the opportunities for us to repent our past transgressions and rid ourselves of unwholesome karma. The best cultivation is to turn our thinking around.

Cultivation in our daily life leads to achievement. Our life will be more complete when we cultivate, for such effort can enhance our merit and improve our positive conditions. It is not empty words or a mere formality, but actually applying the Dharma in our everyday life. When we can use words of compassion to inspire others, eyes of compassion to look upon others, expressions of compassion to greet others, hands of compassion to help others, and a heart of compassion to bless others, then we are truly "practicing cultivation!"

Four Ways of Teaching

Once while the Buddha was traveling and teaching the Dharma, a hostile man scolded him for being unproductive since he only traveled from place to place every day speaking the Dharma. The Buddha told him, "I also work; and like a farmer, I cultivate for food." The cultivation the Buddha referred to is teaching sentient beings. The methods the Buddha used to teach were as follows:

1. Faith is the seed. The *Flower Adornment Sutra* says, "Faith is the source of the Way and the mother of all merit, for it nurtures the root of all goodness." In order for people to attain success in the world, they must have firm faith and confidence. With faith, we have the courage to face difficulties, and the strength to take on challenges. Accordingly, we will accept many more opportunities to learn. In teaching sentient beings, the Buddha spread the seeds of faith everywhere he went. As the seeds were planted in people's minds, they sprouted to bloom and bear fruit when the conditions were right. They became the strength sentient beings relied on in dealing with adversity.

2. Cultivation is the seasonable rain. In teaching sentient beings, the Buddha hoped that we could cultivate a compassionate mind and perform acts of tolerance. In addition, he taught that by upholding precepts, practicing charity, reciting the Buddha's name, or practicing Chan, we could gain peace in our body and mind, and distance ourselves from worry. Human minds can be improved and society purified through cultivation. Even the Buddha himself used cultivation to improve himself and further transform society. His merits of cultivation pro-

vide support for others to succeed. Furthermore, his compassion and wisdom help liberate all sentient beings, while the seasonable rain of his cultivation irrigates and nourishes everyone and everything.

3. Wisdom is sunshine. The Buddha employed wisdom and skillful means that were compatible with the mental disposition of sentient beings to spread the truths that he had realized. He used such means to teach truths regarding dependent origination, cause and effect, karma, and emptiness. These truths can guide us out of the darkness of ignorance and bring an end to the suffering resulting from natural and human-made disasters. For instance, the wisdom of emptiness can break through the darkness of greed and eradicate the gloom of anger and hate. The light of wisdom can brighten up the path that liberates us from the cycle of birth and death. Furthermore, the light of wisdom and merit enable sentient beings to leave behind sorrow and suffering and walk on the broad road of the bodhi path. Like sunshine shining through the darkness and a wind clearing away an unpleasant smell, wisdom allows us to progress toward brightness and clarity.

4. A sense of shame is the good earth. *The Bequeathed Teachings of the Buddha* says, "People with a sense of shame have benevolence. Otherwise, they are no different from animals." A sense of shame is fundamental to improving morals, ridding one's unwholesomeness, and moving toward kindness. It is like the good earth helping all things to grow and mature. The Buddha taught us to be ashamed of our inadequacies. We should be ashamed of not doing enough in supporting our parents, teaching our children, loving our friends and relatives, and contributing to society. With a sense of shame in our hearts, we will not close ourselves off from others with arrogance and self-righteousness, but have the desire and

will to repent our transgressions and progress toward goodness. When we have a sense of shame, we can cultivate harmony and peace between self and others and the world.

The Buddha was not only a farmer good at cultivating the field of the mind, but also an expert in regarding all sentient beings as fields with the potential to bear the fruit of the bodhi. As the ultimate teacher, the Buddha was always active in the deep cultivation of the mind-field of sentient beings and contributed immensely toward purifying society and the human heart.

Repaying Four Debts of Gratitude

In life, we need to appreciate and repay the kindness of others. People who do not understand gratitude are very poor, even though they may have a lot of money and material things. On the other hand, those who repay their debts with gratitude are the wealthiest people in the world. As the saying goes, "In drinking water from the well, we should not forget the well-digger." Even animals repay the love and nurturing of their parents, for crows will feed their parents in return, and lambs will kneel when suckling on the ewe. Buddhism teaches us the "four kindnesses to repay with gratitude," reminding us that these are debts we cannot afford to ignore. These are as follows:

1. We should practice filial piety to express our gratitude for our parents in nurturing us. The kindness of our parents is as high as a mountain and as deep as a river. In *The Book of Odes* [*Shi Jing*], the gratitude we owe our parents is described as "vast as the boundless heavens," and therefore, difficult for us to repay. The *Sutra on the Difficulty of Repaying the Kindness of Parents* [*Fo Shuo Fumu En Zhong Nan Bao Jing*] also mentions the ten kinds of gratitude we owe to our parents, which are extremely deep and broad. How do we repay them? There are three levels to guide us. The first level of filial piety is to support them when they are alive and bury them when they pass away. Bringing honor to the family so that our parents can enjoy the glory of our achievements is the second level. The highest level of filial piety is to guide our parents toward the right faith and away from trouble and worry, so that they can be completely rid themselves of the suffering of the lower realms of existence.

2. We should conduct ourselves with righteousness to repay our gratitude for our teachers in showing us the way to success. Teachers guide us with much patience so that we can gain knowledge and learn etiquette. How do we repay them for teaching us the right way? We need to "take our teachers' resolve as our own and be of one mind with our teachers." We must conduct ourselves with righteousness in benefiting society, bringing into full play what our teachers have taught us. Furthermore, we should even surpass our teacher in learning. In so doing, we can truly repay our gratitude to them.

3. We should be patriotic to express our gratitude to our country for protecting us. Our country is our anchor, providing us with a place to live, as well as protection and haven for our possessions. When we have a country, we can enjoy our rights and be able to establish ourselves in life. The schools, museums, art galleries, and national parks our country has established allow us to learn and enhance our lives. The hospitals, road system, laws, and armed forces provide us with security for our health and livelihood. Therefore, we must love our country and be loyal. We need to have the resolve to serve our country in order to repay our gratitude for the protection and security it offers us.

4. We should support society to repay our gratitude to all sentient beings that help us to succeed in our endeavors. People can live in comfort because of the mutual support sentient beings give one another. Everything in our living environment is the result of the joint efforts of others. For instance, farmers till the land for grain, fruit and vegetables, so as to provide us with sustenance. Workers build houses, roads, and bridges to accommodate us with a place to live and the means to get around. Merchants trade and conduct business to supply us with the daily necessities. Manufacturers produce garments so we can

dress for the weather. Journalists serve us with news and information so that we know what is going on in the world. Train conductors provide us with the convenience of transportation. Therefore, we have to repay our gratitude for society's support in all our endeavors.

People need to have a heart of gratitude in order to repay the community. Those with gratitude in their hearts cherish what they have. It is the most precious virtue of humanity.

Remaining Unmoved by Success or Failure

When we remain calm when facing a crisis, we can gain respect and strengthen ourselves. When we are unmoved by either success or failure, we will be able to live in peace and ease. In conducting ourselves, we must learn to remain calm in the face of change, and more importantly, to be unmoved by either success or failure. The following descriptions will help us to do so.

1. We should not change our attitude in life because of poverty or wealth. In life, our fortunes will inevitably change over time, and we may face difficulties as well as enjoy good situations. Poverty and wealth appear to be opposing terms and states for us to experience, but in reality, they are not absolute. People who are perpetually greedy and discontent with what they have are always poor. On the other hand, those who are happy to give and help others are always wealthy. Therefore, whether someone is rich or poor cannot be evaluated by external riches. It should be based on the intangible wealth of the mind. We should "remain incorruptible by wealth and unmoved by poverty." This means we should not change the way we treat people because of theirs or our momentary wealth or poverty. Such conduct and character are even more precious than money and property.

2. We should not change our state of mind when facing peace or danger. People's emotions often rise and fall with changes in their surroundings. Those who have frequent and unpredictable mood swings will give others the impression of being temperamental and difficult to handle. Therefore, in conducting ourselves we must be able to remain calm and not show our emotions too easily. If we are composed and calm at ordinary times, we

will not lose our poise during emergencies. When we can clearly see the underlying reality of a situation, not react too quickly to external stimuli such as danger, and remain calm and controlled at all times, the depth of our cultivation will be plain for all to see.

3. We should not change our respect for others due to their courteous or rude behavior. Respecting others means recognizing they have something we admire and can learn from. It should not be based on their showing us kindness and treating us well. By the same token, we should not disrespect another because he or she is rude to us and opposes our wishes. In respecting a person, we must praise his or her qualities, such as poise, ethics, knowledge, and abilities. Showing others respect is a basic human value. Therefore, no matter how others treat us, we should not lose our respect for them.

4. We should not let success or failure affect our self-confidence. To be full of confidence with success and disheartened in failure is common for most people. However, for people to achieve major accomplishments, they should not be complacent with small successes, or lose confidence and become passive and pessimistic in face of failure. On the contrary, they should be more courageous when facing more setbacks. For instance, when Thomas Edison's property was completely burned down, he remarked, "I thank the fire for burning down all my previous mistakes." This is someone who had the self-confidence to really achieve great merit and accomplishments.

"Fortune rides on calamity, and calamity is hidden behind fortune." The twists of fate in our life—poverty, wealth, failures, problems, goodness, gains, or losses—are all momentary. If we can look upon them merely as the spice of life and not be bothered by them, our mind will become broad and open, and we will not find ourselves trapped in a dead end.

The Way of Establishing Ourselves

It is better to help ourselves than to seek assistance from others. According to a saying, "It is better to be the [Bodhisattva] Guanyin than to recite or plead with Guanyin." Therefore, we need to be self-reliant. We have to establish ourselves before we can support others. The following are four steps to establishing ourselves:

1. We need more self-reflection before we can be self-awakened. Socrates once said, "An unexamined life is not worth living." The Chinese philosopher Zengzi also said, "We must reflect upon ourselves three times a day." After self-reflection and examination, we will be able to see our minds, actions, and personality. We will see all our shortcomings, such as a very bad temper, excessive greed, and jealousy. Therefore, self-reflection helps us discover our weaknesses and face our conscience, leading to our self-awakening.

2. We need to be self-awakened before we can be self-confident. Once we have self-awareness, we will be able to correct our unwholesome habits. For instance, we can transform greed into joyful giving, anger into compassion, laziness into diligence, and ignorance and wrong views into rationality and right views. After we have corrected our behaviors and thoughts, we can improve our human relationships, making connections with others even though we may not have had so many friends before. If we have the strength to take on duties, we will gain a strong sense of responsibility and be able to shoulder more. In addition, when we are handling more responsibilities, we naturally gain self-confidence. Therefore, with self-awakening, we will also gain in

self-confidence.

3. We need to be self-confident before we can be self-reliant. Self-confidence defines the goals and ideals in life. When we have self-confidence, we can choose on our life's direction. We will be able to plan our future and be in charge of our fate, enabling us to become our own masters. If we are able to fortify ourselves constantly, we will have confidence naturally and be able to apply ourselves fully in whatever we do. Thus, our chance to succeed will be very high. On the contrary, if we lack self-respect and confidence, our life will spiral downward.

4. We need to be self-reliant before we can establish ourselves. In life, we should strive to be self-reliant. According to the saying, "As heaven and earth revolve, the wise should strengthen themselves without ceasing." Moreover, "generals and ministers do not come from any one class; all men should fortify themselves." People who strive and work hard on their own will be able to establish themselves. When we are able to strengthen and establish ourselves, we will live a complete and healthy life.

In order for us to find our place in the world, we must have self-control, establish ourselves, and gain self-reliance. Relying on ourselves is the surest way in life.

Equality and Fairness

People all wish to be treated with equality. However, there are many things in the world that are unfortunately unequal from the very beginning. For instance, there are inequalities between big and small countries, races, and social classes. In addition, there are also distinctions between the wise and foolish, rich and poor, and between the sexes. Therefore, people will often protest inequalities. Buddhism emphasizes equality, for it teaches that "the Buddha and all sentient beings are equal," and "all four castes will assume the name Sakya when they join the monastic order." How do we move from the myriad inequalities in the world to fairness and equality? The following are four ways of doing so:

1. Do not evaluate people's achievements based on their intelligence. A person's intelligence is not the key to success. Success is achieved through diligence and the coming together of the right conditions. For instance, Einstein was considered mentally challenged as a child by his teacher. However, in his pursuit of knowledge and endless exploration into the "unknown," he was able to resolve the questions regarding time and space in the universe. Even those who are diagnosed as being mentally challenged, are still worthy of our respect. We often see mentally challenged people living independently, because they are determined to be treated with dignity. They are actually far superior to people who are physically and mentally able but choose to idle their life away, or worse still, end up resorting to crime. Therefore, we cannot evaluate someone solely on the basis of his or her level of intelligence.

2. Do not judge people's importance by their wealth. Whether or not someone is honorable cannot be judged

according to his or her material wealth and certainly not by his or her looks. Confucius asserted, "If I judged people solely by their looks, I would have missed out on my disciple Ziyu." Similarly, as long as we are willing to progress and improve, poverty is also just a minor interlude in life. In Chinese history, many top entrepreneurs and wealthy tycoons started out very poor in life. They earned their riches through diligence and hard work. Therefore, we cannot judge a person on the basis of material wealth.

3. Do not assess people's honor by their social status. The classic Chinese novel, *The Dream of the Red Chamber* [*Honglou Meng*], observes, "Honor and humiliation have gone in cycles since ancient times." This implies that no one remains a laborer or a president forever. Differences in position at work alone should not indicate a high or low status, for even janitors or laborers perform work that is essential to society. The renowned Chinese artist Qi Baishi has said, "An official may look very dignified in his uniform. When pushed over, he is just a pile of mud." The uniform signifies a certain position, but the person wearing it is basically no different from anyone else. Therefore, we should not assess anyone by his or her social status.

4. Do not distinguish between self and others in terms of gain and loss. The *Sutra on the Treasury of Truth* asserts, "Victory breeds vengeance, and loss brings self-degradation. With no intention to win or lose, we gain peace without fighting with others." Most people like to compete with others in their attempt to see who is best. Once they start comparing and competing, they will distinguish who is superior and inferior, and conflicts over fame and gain will soon follow. On the other hand, if people are mindful of their being part of the whole community, they will have mutual respect for one another and

support each other in their endeavors. Over the ages, many who craved power fought against one another, wasting much energy and resources. What do their victories and defeats matter to anyone today? "The Great Wall still stands, but the First Emperor of the Qin (the emperor who built it) is nowhere to be seen." Therefore, we should not waste our precious time in life by distinguishing between self and others in terms of gain and loss.

As long as we are not calculating and petty, we will have few conflicts. What is most important is for us to have a calm and fair mind that does not discriminate against others.

On Knowledge

When we learn something every day, we gain wisdom. Wisdom helps us navigate life, and acquiring knowledge is the beginning of wisdom. Therefore, we all have to pursue knowledge. There are many kinds of knowledge in this world, and people have different preferences for them. For instance, people may be interested in science, medicine, art, or literature. The various fields and subjects all have their own fields of learning and knowledge. The accumulation of knowledge does not solely come with age. Knowledge is also based on reading broadly and thinking openly and critically. The following are definitions of knowledge:

1. Scholarship is the knowledge of theory. One researches by reading different theories and ways of thinking. Einstein's theory of relativity and Darwin's theory on evolution are examples of important theories. We may also study the Bible, Buddhist sutras, various encyclopedias, and Confucian teachings contained within *The Four Books* [*Si Shu*] and *The Five Classics* [*Wu Jing*]. These areas of scholarship represent the knowledge of reasoning and theory.

2. Thinking is the knowledge of application. Confucians stated, that "learning without thinking is pointless." Knowledge from books needs to be assimilated before we can know how to apply it. Regarding the path towards wisdom, Buddhism advocates "Entering samadhi with listening, contemplating, and practicing." Through reflection, we can assimilate knowledge so that it becomes practical wisdom. It is like singing; after we have sung a song a thousand times, we do not need any coaching and can sing it quite well.

3. Judgment is the knowledge of assessment. We need to

know the difference between right and wrong, good and bad, kindness and harm in the world. We should be able to assess priorities and make the right judgments. We cannot afford to be ambiguous with right and wrong all the time and uncertain about everything. Buddhism affirms the equality of all phenomena, which is from a theoretical point of view. The nature of all things is empty, and therefore, transcends any duality in form. However, from a worldly point of view, all phenomena are as varied and different as their number. One is one and two is two, just as mountains are mountains and water is water. We can never get them confused.

4. Wisdom is the knowledge of enlightenment. No matter how much knowledge there is in the world, if we do not appreciate it with our mind and spirit, it is no more than words on paper. At best, it can only be a form of study. Often, in pursuing knowledge or listening to people talk, we will respond, "I get it!" But do we truly understand? If we are asked to repeat it, we may say we don't know, which means that we do not really understand. In Buddhism, we must truly know the Way for it to become imprinted in our minds. When we truly understand something, we can appreciate its meaning and transform it into wisdom. This is the knowledge of enlightenment.

Knowledge is worldly intelligence which we can seek externally. Prajna-wisdom is developing internally the Buddha Nature that each person has inherently. In learning or dealing with matters, knowledge and scholarship cannot resolve all the problems. It is only through opening the capacity of our minds that we can develop prajna-wisdom in order to tell what is right from what is wrong, and thereby transform ignorance into enlightenment.

The Way of Tolerance

In order to gain any achievement in society, people need various qualities. For instance, superior knowledge, expansive ambition, a broad mind, and tolerance are the greatest assets for the difficult path of life. Among them, tolerance is a cultivation that we particularly cannot afford to neglect. Tolerance is not retreating. It is applying a balanced mind in equanimity when faced with the unfair situations in the world. The way to tolerance is defined as follows:

1. Hold our tongue, and trouble will find no place to grow. According to a proverb, "A restless sky brings rain; a restless person brings trouble." When people are angry, they easily lose their reason and get into trouble. How do we refrain from getting angry? Besides being reasonable, we have to exercise patience and tolerance. Tolerance begins with our mouth, and progresses to our countenance, and finally, our heart. It can also generate internal strength. With strength, we will not be bogged down by worries or negative thoughts, and we will not become angry. "When we can swallow our anger, the winds and waves will remain calm." On the other hand, "Lack of patience in small matters spoils great undertakings." Consequently, there will be peace if we can tolerate others.

2. Spare others and do not argue with them. "If we forgive others when we are right, we are magnanimous. Magnanimity broadens the road. When we are unreasonable and hurt others, we are overbearing. Being overbearing narrows our path." Some people enjoy arguing with others, even over a sentence, and often pursue a point relentlessly when they feel they are right. In real-

ity, it is better to leave some room for others to save face. This will make it easier for one another when there is the chance to meet again in the future. Even though the other person may have wronged us in different ways, if we forgive him or her and let it go, maybe someday that person will help us in return. Therefore, in forgiving others, we are actually giving space to ourselves. We should never fight with others just to win, because winning an argument does not necessarily mean we are superior.

3. Being patient for a moment, and the fire pit will turn into a lotus pond. Mountains are steep, and oceans rough. Most things in life are a disappointment. So if we want to succeed in our career, we cannot always expect smooth sailing. "Without a chilling cold, how can the plum blossoms perfume the air; with a sweltering heat wave, even the centers of the flowers in the lotus pond are fragrant." Only those people who can withstand setbacks and persevere to the end can succeed. Like lotus flowers, the more intense the heat, the more fragrantly they bloom. Therefore, in life, we must be able to endure the cold ice and snow in winter, as well as the heat and sweat of summer.

4. Take a step back, and the path of cultivation in the world will open. Farmers planting rice seedlings must move backwards step by step in order to complete their job. In our cultivation and work in this world, we also need to appreciate the philosophy of taking a step back. "Moving forward is not always as beneficial as stepping back." Sometimes, when we retreat one step, the sky and ocean will become open and wide. If we take a step back, we can turn around and see the other shore. We must know how to turn around, and not wait till we hit the wall and regret it when we bruise our face. Such is the path of cultivation in our world.

We all experience both smooth sailing and setbacks in life.

When we are doing well, we should treasure the moment but not lose our focus. In facing life's inevitable setbacks, we need to be patient. When we are patient, we will be able to get through anything. Therefore, if we have ideals and want to create our future, we must learn to tolerate others before we can reach our goals.

Merits of Giving

Buddhism teaches that in pursuing good fortune, people need to start with giving. Giving can be classified into several types. There is the giving of material wealth; the giving of the Dharma, such as bestowing upon others knowledge, skill, and the truth; and the giving of "fearlessness" through supporting and protecting righteousness and the truth so that people will no longer be afraid. The merits of giving are like sowing seeds. When a seed is sowed in the soil and cultivated with water and fertilizer, it will be able to grow well and bear plenty of fruit. According to a Buddhist verse, "It is best to cultivate merit inside the gates of the Triple Gem, give a dollar and reap ten thousand in return. Emperor Liang was a living example. He gave away his straw hat and ruled the kingdom in return." This is the best proof of the merit of giving. The following are some more illustrations:

1. By giving others life, one can gain longevity. Longevity is something people all wish for. However, even if someone is as wealthy as a nation, there is no way such a person can buy long life. By the same token, neither can anyone in high positions, such as presidents or emperors, extend their lives. So how do we gain longevity and good fortune? According to the *Sutra on the Five Merits of Giving* [*Fo Shuo Shishi Huo Wu Fubao Jing*], "Those who give others life will enjoy longevity and not be met with injury or sudden death." Giving others life means to refrain from killing, and to release trapped animals or protect animal rights. In the *Sutra of Parables* [*Piyu Jing*], it is recorded that a novice monk saved a colony of ants and ended up extending his own life. "Sow a melon seed, and one reaps melons; sow a bean, and one reaps beans." If we want to live a long

life, not only do we have to help the needy but also practice compassion and refrain from killing. When we sow
the causes of cherishing and protecting life, then naturally we will reap the fruit of long life.

2. By giving others positive appearances, one can gain dignified physical features. This includes giving others
food so that they are healthy and no longer thin and pale-
faced. Also by giving others clothing, they can look
decent, and are no longer undignified or embarrassed in
rags. *The Dharma Garden of Buddhism* [*Fayuan Zhulin*]
states, "Those who give others positive looks will enjoy
dignified features for many lives. Their colors will be
bright and rosy, and people will be happy to see them."
When we give others clothes, food, medicine, and other
daily necessities, they can live in good health and have a
pleasant appearance. They will no longer suffer the pains
of hunger, thirst, poverty, and sickness. In turn, we too
will gain the fruit of dignified physical features.

3. By giving others comfort, one can gain fearlessness.
Giving others comfort is to allow them to live life in
comfort. For instance, when we provide the homeless
with housing and bedding, they will no longer suffer
from the heat and cold of living on the streets. When
people lose their homes because of unemployment, high
rent, hurricanes or earthquakes, we can supply them with
shelter so they do not have to worry about where they
will stay, and be supplied with basic necessities. When
others are in trouble and do not know what to do, we can
comfort them so they can have some peace of mind and
no longer be fearful. The merit of giving others comfort
will in turn bring us peace and harmony in life without
fear or anxiety.

4. By giving others strength, one can gain triumph over
matters. Giving others strength means serving others and
helping them accomplish what they are doing. For

instance, when we see others failing in their career, we should encourage them so they have the strength to start over. When others are uncertain about their future, not knowing where to go, we should show our concern and counsel them so they do not feel lonely, thereby enabling them to gain the courage to move on. Therefore, by giving others strength, we will be able to triumph in what we do.

Giving does not necessarily entail just giving money. Sometimes a few kind words on someone's behalf can allow incredible causes and conditions to materialize for him or her. It can even be a small amount of food that can provide hope for others, or the strength to turn their life around. Sometimes even a casual smile can give people a warm feeling. Therefore, the merits of giving are limitless.

Accepting and Forgiving

People all have strengths and shortcomings. Therefore, in getting along with others, we should pay attention to their virtues and not their faults. We must be able to make use of their strengths and forgive and tolerate their shortcomings. Thus, there is no one in the world we cannot work with and make good use of his or her skills. The following are some keys to what to accept and forgive.

1. Accept people's naiveté and forgive their foolishness. Sometimes we may meet people who are very straightforward and do not seem very bright or skilled. We should appreciate their honesty and righteousness, and tolerate their foolishness. We can assign them uncomplicated work that does not require them to deal with changes. They just need to take orders to do a good job.

2. Accept people's simplicity and forgive their awkwardness. Some people are naturally down to earth and unskilled in using flowery language to please others, but they will remain steadfast in their job. We need to forgive their awkwardness and appreciate their simplicity. For someone to be able to retain his or her simple nature is certainly commendable.

3. Accept people's rigidity and forgive their attachment. Some people are very strict in what they do and inflexible in their behavior. People like that may sometimes be too attached to their views. However, they are not easily tempted by gain and tend to work in a righteous and just manner. As long as we can tolerate their attachments, they are worthy of our trust in giving them major responsibilities.

4. Accept people's agility and forgive their negligence. There are people who are skillful and can respond to sit-

uations swiftly. They not only act quickly but also are able to think just as fast. However, in the pursuit of being fast, they sometimes fail to cover all the bases either in how they speak or deal with matters. We need to forgive their occasional negligence and make good use of their agility, so as to bring their talents into full play.

5. Accept people's articulateness and forgive their unruliness. Some people are very clear about the differences between right and wrong, kind and harmful, or good and bad. Moreover, they are often outspoken about issues. It is inevitable that they are sometimes viewed as being arrogant and unruly. However, we should never reject them for being outspoken or disorderly. We should accept their verbal abilities and the purpose they serve in raising others' awareness to issues.

6. Accept people's trustworthiness and forgive their cautiousness. There are people who consider trust their top priority and conduct themselves accordingly. Because of their over-emphasis on trust and keeping promises, they may sometimes fail to nurture harmonious human relationships. In addition, they do not know how to adjust according to changing conditions and give others the impression of being too cautious and conservative. We must accept their discretion and commend their valuing trust and keeping of promises.

All in all, it is impossible for people to be perfect in everything. We all have shortcomings as well as strengths. According to the saying, "There is certainly a use for one's inborn talents." Therefore, we should not dismiss ourselves too easily. Similarly, we cannot jump to conclusions, making rash judgments and condemning others. Instead, we should accept their strengths and excuse their shortcomings.

What Is Chan?

Buddhism often teaches people to practice Chan. In reality, Chan is not in the sole domain of Buddhism, for it is in the heart and mind of every person. Since we all have a heart and mind, we should all embody Chan. What is Chan? The following are some definitions:

1. Moving firewood and carrying water are Chan. Chan is not "the eyes observing the nose and the nose watching the mind." It is not simply about sitting on a cushion or "an old monk in deep concentration." Chan is present in daily work. For instance, in moving firewood, carrying water, doing chores and other services, the here and now is Chan. When we are able to perform every chore with skill and concentration, experience the meaning of work, and cultivate patience within a job, we will have realized Chan. Therefore, in doing a minor chore like moving firewood or carrying water, this is Chan.

2. Walking, standing, sitting, and sleeping are Chan. Chan can be found in sitting quietly as well as in action. There is Chan in sitting or walking meditation, and it is also present while we are eating or sleeping. In our everyday life, when we can calm our mind and focus on the daily activities, be it sitting, walking, or resting, and not be influenced by our surroundings, we will be able to experience Chan. Therefore, putting on clothes or eating a meal is also Chan. When we can abide in Chan in our daily living, it will be like "the moon outside the window is the same, but when there are plum blossoms it will be different." If we have Chan in life, the flavor of life will taste different.

3. Expediency and ingenuity are Chan. Chan is not rigid or

dull. It is not confined by following old rules. Chan is lively, humorous, and expedient. Every facial expression, look, and gesture of the Chan masters and cultivated practitioners in the past were filled with Chan. Their every word, act, view, and thought embodied the Middle Path. For them, each blade of grass and tree, and in every grain of sand and clumps of rock were the mind of Chan. Therefore, when we have a mind of Chan, we can see Chan in the world, nature, and all phenomena, for they are full of ingenious wonders.

4. Accepting adversities willingly is Chan. In life, we can experience both smooth sailing and setbacks. When we are able to face both successes and obstacles with an "unmoving mind" or calmness, we have Chan. Are you able to apply the same mind to the hustle and bustle of everyday life? When you can, you know what Chan is.

What is Chan? It is cultivation and life. When we can experience the joy of Chan and the Dharma in living, we will have found the true cultivation. It is also the practice advocated by Humanistic Buddhism.

The World of Chan

Buddhism speaks about the "Ten Dharma Realms." Humans have their own world, and so do heavenly and hellish beings, hungry ghosts, and animals. While the beings within the "Six Common and Four Sagely Realms" all have their own planes of existence, within the realm of humans, the world of each individual is different. Some people only think about material goods, and they reside in the world of money. Similarly, some people may dwell in love or busy themselves in the world of fame and fortune. The truth is that objectively the world is the same for everyone. It is only one's individual state of mind that is different. Like scholars having their own world, Chan practitioners also have theirs. What is the world of Chan like? Here are four definitions:

1. The world of Chan is a moment and is also everlasting. In the world of Chan, a moment is not short and a kalpa is not long. This is what is meant by "a thought embracing 3,000 realms." A moment can last endless kalpas and be everlasting, because within the world of Chan, there is no longer the duality of big or small, have or have-not, long or short, far or near, self or other. Within the world of the Chan practitioner, one is everything, and everything within the dharma realms is completely harmonized. Therefore, a moment is also everlasting.

2. The world of Chan is small and also great. It is "a world within a flower, a Tathagata within a leaf." In the world of Chan, a flower, a leaf, a grain of sand or a rock encompasses the limitless dharma realm. Therefore, "Mt. Sumeru embraces a mustard seed; a mustard seed contains Mt. Sumeru." Because a tiny mustard seed can contain Mt. Sumeru, the world of Chan is both small and great.

3. The world of Chan is affliction and bodhi. Most people think afflictions are afflictions, and bodhi is bodhi. The reality is that "affliction is bodhi," for without afflictions, no bodhi can be attained. It is like the pineapples and persimmons that are very sour and bitter before they ripen. However, after weathering the elements of wind, sunshine, rain, and dew, they become very sweet when ripe. Where does the sweetness come from? From the sourness and bitterness. Therefore, affliction is bodhi because the latter cannot be sought anywhere else. When we transform our afflictions into bodhi, it is like changing sourness and bitterness into sweetness.

4. The world of Chan is the cycle of birth and death as well as nirvana. Birth and death are the realities of life, but most people avoid talking about death. In reality, death is not to be feared because true life does not die; it is the physical body that dies. Our true nature, Dharma-body, and life of wisdom are not subject to the cycle of birth and death. Therefore, in the world of a Chan practitioner, life is everlasting and does not die. It always abides in nirvana, and remains unmoved. That is true life.

Chan transcends all duality and sees all as equal. In the perception of a Chan practitioner, there is no long or short, big or small, pure or defiled, arising or ceasing.

Dealing with Matters with a Chan Mind

Wherever people live, there will be issues; and where there are issues, there will be questions of right and wrong. If we can look after our own mind well, we will not be bothered by the right and wrong arising between self and others. Therefore, in dealing with matters, we need a Chan mind. We need to use our limited lifetime to seek what is limitless. We should not waste our precious time in life bickering over some minor right and wrong between people. The following are four points about how to use a Chan mind in dealing with matters:

1. When setbacks occur, we should not blame others or have complaints. What we have in life is not necessarily the result of an easy time. When setbacks arrive, what do we do? We should not complain or blame others. "In appreciating causes and effects, we will not complain about heaven; in understanding ourselves, we will not blame others." However, even with some minor disappointments, people will complain about heaven and earth, and blame their family and friends for what happens. In complaining and blaming, we are only exposing ourselves as being weak and incapable. Cultivated people with abilities will never complain or blame anyone, because they know it will only make matters worse.

2. When sickness comes, we should have no fear or anxiety. Humans subsist on grains and other staples, and it is inevitable that we will get sick. However, most people are fearful of sickness. As the saying goes, "even heroes fear nothing except the torture of sickness." Buddhism speaks about "practitioners needing to be thirty-percent ill," because if we suffer some minor physical pain and sickness sometimes, it can enhance our resolve for the

Way. This then becomes the basis of our motivation to progress and cultivate ourselves. What is important is mental health. When we are suffering from sickness, we need to have the right view that our physical body is only a combination of the four elements and five aggregates of existence. We should do as the *Heart Sutra* [*Prajnaparamitahrdaya Sutra*] teaches, "Contemplating the emptiness of the five aggregates of existence." Then, naturally, we will be able to transcend all suffering and be without fear and anxiety. We can distance ourselves from all delusions and gain equanimity and liberation.

3. When slander arises, we should not defend ourselves or be troubled. "Only the mediocre will not be the object of envy." In this Saha world in which we live, most people who are successful will inevitably suffer criticism and slander. Even the Buddha was harmed by Devadatta, and Jesus was betrayed by his disciple. When we are slandered and hurt, it is very important that we do not defend ourselves or try to explain. We need not be troubled because all gossip ceases with wisdom. We need only conduct ourselves correctly. When others tease or ridicule us, it is because of the "manure" in their minds. If we are wise, we will not be upset.

4. When honor comes, we should not be arrogant. The greatest failure in life is arrogance, for arrogance brings peril. Therefore, if we are given extreme honor and fortune, we should not be conceited about our achievements. Frequently, fortune and disaster come hand in hand in this world, while failure often hides in the shadow of success. Therefore, not only should we remain humble in our victory, we should also know how to yield to others in our position. "We should cautiously reflect upon ourselves if we are given superior fortune and honor, then our position will become secure." Therefore, in conducting ourselves, we should be open-minded and

as humble as the great earth capable of carrying all living things and accomplishing all matters.

There is something within each of us more precious than gold or diamonds. It is our inherent Buddha Nature. Buddha Nature, expressed in simpler terms, is the Chan mind. When we use the Chan mind to deal with both successes and failures, we will live peacefully at all times.

The Four Most Supreme Dharmas

The Discourses of the Buddha [*Agama Sutras*] are reportedly the earliest Buddhist sutras and also the basis of the most important concepts of original Buddhism. These sutras are filled with the teachings and spirit of Humanistic Buddhism. There are four divisions to the *Discourses*: *The Long Discourses of the Buddha* [*Dirghagama Sutra*], *The Middle Length Discourses of the Buddha* [*Madhyamagama Sutra*], *The Gradual Discourses of the Buddha* [*Ekottarikagama Sutra*], and *The Connected Discourses of the Buddha* [*Samyuktagama Sutra*]. In *The Long Discourses of the Buddha*, there is a section on the "four most supreme Dharmas," meaning there are four things in the Dharma that are most important for us in life. The following are their definitions:

1. Those who give gain fortune. When we talk about giving, most people will consider it as giving to others. The truth is that in giving, the one who benefits the most is ourselves. Giving is like sowing seeds, for there will certainly be a harvest later on. It is the most reliable form of investment. Whether it is giving money, the Dharma, or security, we are assured of fortune and merit. These kinds of giving are also called cultivating the fields of merit. In Buddhism, it is said, "among the eight fields of merit, caring for the sick ranks first." It also states, "according to the differences of intent in the mind-field, the effect will be differentiated as either superior or inferior." In reality, whether it is for the virtuous sages, our parents, the needy, or the sick, as long as we have sincerity in giving, it will be the supreme field of merit. In giving, we demonstrate we are wealthy and have the resources to do so. If we rely on others to give to us every day, we are certainly poor and lacking.

Therefore, we should be happy in giving, because the more we give, the more we gain.

2. Those who have compassion are without resentment. Compassion is the foundation of Buddhism, so it is also called the religion of compassion. A compassionate mind is the foundation for all living beings to live endlessly. It also is a demonstration of the bright side of human nature. Compassion is the best medicine to cure the sickness of anger. The endless conflicts between people and ongoing wars among countries are all the result of anger. A thought of compassion can resolve hate and anger. If we always bear a compassionate mind in speaking, conducting ourselves, and dealing with people and situations, we will not make any enemies and we will eagerly engage in whatever we do. We will bear no grudges: "With one compassionate person, all people will accompany such a person; with ten thousand compassionate people, all dharma realms will be as one."

3. Those who practice benevolence can reduce harm. The sutras state, "Each and every arising thought of individuals and sentient beings is all karma." There is wholesome, unwholesome, and neutral karma. Once we commit either wholesome or unwholesome karma, we will create a corresponding effect, and so it is said, "For unwholesome causes sowed, a corresponding retribution will arise. We cannot do good deeds to neutralize what we deserve." However, there is a special practice in Buddhism, in which the practice of repentance and benevolence can lighten the burden of unwholesome retribution. Also, we can create more wholesome conditions to strengthen our benevolence so as to mature wholesome retribution, and at the same time, weaken the power of the unwholesome conditions. It is like a glass of salt water, for if we add the plain water of positive causes, we can dilute the saltiness of unwholesome retri-

bution. Just like cultivating a field of seedlings, if we keep irrigating and fertilizing the plants, they will grow strong and big. Then, even though there may be some weeds in between, the adverse impact will not be so strong. Therefore, having unwholesome karma is not fearful, because most importantly, we can practice more benevolent deeds. When we have enough positive causes and conditions, we can thereby reduce our unwholesome karma.

4. Those who are not attached to desires have no worries. The many desires people have every day are solely based on the gratification of their senses amidst the deluded dust of this world. However, "the ocean of desire is difficult to fill," and there will never be a day when desires are fully satisfied. Therefore, the more desires we have, the more trouble we will have. Moreover, in the pursuit of sensual pleasures, we create the fruit of suffering that results from our unwholesome karma. Therefore, the sensual pleasures of the world can only be considered as half pleasure and half suffering. Because sensual pleasures are tainted, temporary, and uncertain, so the virtuous sages since ancient times admonished us not to indulge in lust and desire. While Buddhism does not require people to abstain completely from their desires, they should be well guided. The waves and currents of the ocean of desire should be directed toward the right direction. In other words, we should pursue the "desire for positive dharmas" and stay away from "tainted ones." When we distance ourselves from inappropriate and tainted desires, we will be far from the bonds of trouble and worry. What liberation and ease that will be!

The Dharma is supreme among the Triple Gem of the Buddha, the Dharma, and the Sangha (the community of practitioners). The Dharma is the truth of life and the universe, as well as the boat of compassion that helps us to attain liberation. "Rely on ourselves; rely on the Dharma; and do not rely upon anything else." Therefore, the "four most supreme Dharmas" as described in *The Long Discourses of the Buddha*, should become our standard in life.

Developing Ourselves

In constructing a new building, we need to develop the land before we can start work. When we establish a factory, we have to develop new products to remain competitive. Farmers explore new hybrids in order to increase their harvest. There are many countries in the world making use of land reclaimed from the ocean to build airports and industrial parks. They also open up land to plant orchards and farms. It seems that the whole world is developing and exploring. However, what we really need to do is develop ourselves, because we have endless treasures within waiting for us to explore. How can we develop ourselves? The following four keys explain how this is done:

1. We must know ourselves well. If we lack self-awareness, we will be confused, not knowing the resources and wealth we already possess. Therefore, self-awareness is very important. But how do we enhance it? First, we need to enrich our knowledge in every field and enhance our cultivation of morals. More importantly, we should have right judgment so that we can assess ourselves seriously and reflect upon ourselves deeply. Then, we will be able to make the right choices along our journey in life. Therefore, we need to maintain self-awareness during every moment of life.

2. We must be self-assured. Sentient beings have been endlessly transmigrating between the six planes of existence. Gradually, they have forgotten about their inherent Buddha Nature and believed that they were just common beings. If we can develop our Buddha Nature and become confident that, "Buddha is me; and I am the Buddha," we will not perform any bad deeds when we have the Buddha in our hearts. Therefore, we have to be

self-assured and set goals for ourselves, so as to create our own worth, which will lead to the expansion of our own possibilities.

3. We must be able to shoulder responsibility. If we do not have the courage to take on any responsibility, we will not succeed at anything. Conversely, those who have the strength to bear responsibilities can accept challenges and the trials of tribulation. When people have a sense of responsibility, they will be actively committed to their career and face the challenges of adversity. They will not blame the heavens or others around them for any misfortunes, and they will also be able to get along well with others. People who can shoulder responsibilities have confidence in themselves. They are the ones who can truly realize the meaning of life.

4. We must develop ourselves. People need to have the intention to develop themselves before they can progress and open up their lives. We must know our potential in order to do so. When we discover our inadequacies, we must adapt to our circumstances, but at the same time, we must keep strengthening ourselves with new ideas, technology, and knowledge. Besides consistently working hard to address our shortcomings, we have to develop our talents and skills by being actively involved in serving the community. In this way, we will be able to craft a beautiful and benevolent life for ourselves.

Practicing Buddhism is about developing our true mind and our Buddha Nature. People who know how to develop their innate resources are truly wise and wealthy.

Developing Potential

We all have limitless potential, like the many minerals buried deep in the mountains such as gold, silver, bronze, and iron. Sometimes, because people are lazy or do not know their inherent gifts, they thus fail to develop their potential. This is really regrettable! Actually, our life depends on how we explore and develop the limitless potential inside of us. The following ways will develop our potential:

1. We can expand our physical potential through training. For instance, we can increase how much we are able to carry through strength training. In lifting weights, some people can only start with twenty, thirty, or fifty pounds. However, as they train over time, they can lift a hundred or two hundred pounds. This is how one develops potential. After this potential is developed, our bodies will be able to carry more weight. Moreover, we can also train gradually in developing other skills in areas such as swimming, running, or rock climbing. Therefore, physical potential can be tapped through training, allowing us to carry more or go farther.

2. We can increase our mental potential to make judgments and decisions. Some people have a very sharp mind, while others are slower in reacting to situations. We can also develop our mental potential through training our mind. For instance, we can often ask ourselves, "Why?" and go on to think of the answer. As we keep asking and answering our own questions, we will one day open up our minds and gain understanding. When we have wisdom and good reasoning, we will be able to bring our mental potential into full play, enabling us to tell right from wrong and decide what to give and what to take.

Therefore, mental potential can be developed to make good judgments and decisions.

3. We can extend our emotional potential to become more considerate of others and willing to sacrifice for them. Some people are more sensitive emotionally, while others are more rational and emphasize reasoning. Of course, it is best if we are rational and can still be sensitive at the same time. People who are sensitive are easily moved and can generate empathy for the suffering of others. They are considerate of those around them and often look at matters from a humanistic point of view. It is thus easy for them to get the approval and support of others. We all have the potential to be sensitive. This involves training ourselves to have compassion, patience, and consideration for others, and to practice making sacrifices and contributions. When we develop our emotional potential, we are more likely to commit ourselves to serving and benefiting all sentient beings.

4. We can train our mental potential to become enlightened to life. Where are the true treasures in life? They are right inside our very mind. Our mind-field has endless treasures and potential, representing the Buddha Nature inside each of us. If we can develop our inherent potential, we can become enlightened to life. We can distance ourselves from worry and realize endless life beyond birth or death. Thus, our mental potential can help us become enlightened to life.

People all have endless potential. There are many marathon runners, world-class swimmers, and mountain climbers, as well as many people with extraordinary skills. They are able to develop their potential and bring it into full play, which distinguishes them from ordinary people. Thus, anyone who can develop his or her potential is truly a capable person.

Mottoes for Facing the World

How to get along with others and handle matters are the major lessons we need to learn in life. Some people may live to be eighty years old but still fail to appreciate the skills in dealing with worldly matters. Nowadays, there are even specialists who study the philosophy of how to face the world. The following four mottoes explain how to deal with people and matters in life.

1. Take a step back; the sea and sky are open and clear. We have a world in front of us and also another when we retreat. The world of advancing is often vigorous, but the one behind us is broader. It is only by clearly seeing these two worlds that we can truly have a complete life. We do not have to take every step forward because while there is half of our world in front of us, there is another half behind if we would just turn around and look. Therefore, in taking a step back, we will find an open sea and a clear sky.

2. Yield a little bit and be at peace. In conducting ourselves, "we should not take a backseat in the face of righteousness; we should not charge ahead in face of gain." According to the saying, "How peaceful one can be by retreating three steps in the face of fame and fortune, and how relaxed and at ease one can be by being patient in the face of gossip concerning self and others." Therefore, we should not demand a hundred percent from others, because we can actually gain more when we yield a bit to them instead. Knowing how to yield to others brings real peace and harmony.

3. Be patient with what others say and be worry-free. The arguments and conflicts between people are often the result of unintentional verbal offense. Because of a few

simple words, people get involved in big fights, which may even turn violent and out of control. The truth is that speech is often just mere words and one's intention may be quite different. When we think positively upon hearing something, then we can accept it as encouragement, but if we think negatively, we take it as criticism. We cannot demand others to speak well all the time, so if we can just turn our own thinking around, we would no longer be troubled. In this age of democracy, many different voices are allowed to air their views. Therefore, the more we can have patience with what others say, the more we can be worry-free.

4. Be patient for a moment and experience joy and ease. For a flower to blossom requires many conditions. A seed must be buried deep in the soil to germinate, putting up with the darkness, moisture, and loneliness. Even when the flower blooms, it still has to withstand the wind, frost, rain, and snow, as well as any harm the bees may cause while gathering nectar for honey. In the end, the flower can truly blossom fully, showing its color and shape. In conducting ourselves, we need to put up with blame and injustice, in order to achieve success and improve our morality. Therefore, when faced with difficulties, we must not be impulsive for sometimes we have to be patient. We should not consider tolerance a disadvantage. Being patient is for the moment only, but the resulting joy and ease may last a long time.

These principles for facing the world serve to remind us to take a step backward in what we do, and stop to think. When we are humble, patient, and yielding to others, we will be able to avoid conflict. If we can all keep this in mind, then we can hope to find benefit as we conduct ourselves.

Connecting All with One

In *The Analects of Confucius*, Confucius told his disciple Zigong that his broad and deep knowledge came from "connecting all with one." The truths about every matter in the world are actually interconnected. "By grasping one truth, everything will be clear." By understanding how one thing works and applying it to different situations, we will appreciate how everything functions. Thus, the renowned Chinese scholar Cheng Yi said, "From within ourselves, we can appreciate the truth of all phenomena." The following illustrations explain how we can connect all matters with one principle.

1. All dishonest people are inevitably hypocritical in their flattery. The scholar Ouyang Xiu said, "Gentlemen make friends with gentlemen based on morals; the petty make friends with the petty based on profit." The latter are always greedy for fame and fortune. They are hypocritical, since their speech is flattering and their behavior cunning. Once they meet people with power and money, they latch onto them through flattery. Such is the conduct of petty people. The ancients said, "Petty people follow their cravings." Their smooth relationship with others is motivated by their desire for personal profit. They speak words of honey but always bear a knife within, ready at any time to deal harm to others. Therefore, we must be cautious in dealing with such people.

2. All rivers are inevitably winding. It is impossible for the creeks, brooks, streams, and rivers of the world to flow straight all the way. They flow from their origins high up in the mountains, and coming across obstacles such as rocks and trees, they branch out. Or if there are interlocking hills and valleys, they will wind around them as they flow. Therefore, we sometimes describe rivers as bent and crooked like slithering snakes. So too is our

life: no one in this world can finish the journey of life so smoothly each step of the way, unobstructed by wind and waves. However, if we can be like rivers, we can still seek new ways and channels in spite of the obstacles. As we progress with courage, we need have no fear that we cannot reach our destination.

3. All trees in a forest inevitably support one another. According to the saying, "A single shred of silk does not make a thread; a single tree does not make a forest." When numerous trees support and embrace each other, they can form a great forest. Behind every success in this world, there are always the fruition of various causes and conditions. For instance, our ancestors developed land, and kings and emperors founded dynasties. In addition, all the daily necessities we need in life, such as the founding of a business enterprise, the establishment of a family, or the cooking a meal, are the result of the cooperation and hard work of many people.

4. All peace and joy comes from being carefree. The source of happiness is not material pleasures, nor is it found in the praise of others or how much wealth we possess. Joy in life comes from being carefree. Avalokitesvara Bodhisattva is called in Chinese "Guanzizai," which means "observing and carefree." In observing people, events, circumstances, and the mind, Avalokitesvara can appreciate the empty nature of them all, and thus becomes carefree. If we too can be this way, we will not be anxious or remorseful. We will not be afraid of loss, greed, or desire. Consequently, we will be able to live in grace and contentment. Life lacks peace when we are not carefree, and so if we want peace and joy, we must first seek a carefree mind.

If we can apply the truth of "connecting with one" in life, we can certainly connect with all truths in the world. This will enable us to devise strategies to win any battle, even when we are a thousand miles away.

Half and Half

The world is full of wonders, but everything comes in half and half. For instance, half of the people are men and the other half women; half of them are good and the other half not so good; and half the time is day and the other half night. Living in this "half-and-half" world, it is almost impossible or very difficult for us to achieve one hundred percent perfection. Therefore, we can only make use of this "half" of life to influence the other half, like trying to affect the bad half with the good. The following views explain the half-and-half life we live.

1. Life is filled with half joy and half sorrow. Laozi once said, "Fortune rides on calamity, and calamity is hidden behind fortune." There is no one in the world who is forever happy or sad. Our life is sometimes joyful and other times sorrowful. They are like day and night taking turns after one another. Only people who can adapt to situations can make good use of both the light and the dark, happiness and sorrow. The ancients said, "How can all matters under the heavens be according to people's wishes. It is only when our minds are at peace that we can deal with self and others. We can then follow circumstances and live at ease." Most people are focused on the gains and losses of life, and become happy or sad as the impermanence of worldly matters dictates. Consequently, they are never able to find peace. If we are content with our lot in life, we will be able to face all adversity. We will be like Confucius, whose "happiness led him to forget his worries," and our minds will be liberated from the fetters of sorrow and pain.

2. Gains and losses of fame and fortune are half and half. It is not easy for people to gain both fame and fortune at the

same time, given that such worldly matters are half and half and are relative to one another. If we are inextricably caught in the net of fighting for fame and fortune, we may indeed lose more than we gain. Some entrepreneurs may have built an empire with their corporate enterprises, but lost the love of their family and their own health in exchange. The ruler of a country may keep waging war in order to gain more territory, yet end up losing the support of his citizens as well as his precious character and moral standards. Laozi asked, "What is dearer, fame or our body? What is more, our body or goods? What is worse, gain or death?" The value of life depends on how we evaluate it. Between the gains and losses over fame and fortune, we must be wise in how we assess them.

3. The gathering and dispersing of wealth is half and half. We are often witness to the major ups and downs in people's lives. So too does their wealth come and go: in the blink of an eye, they could be living with immense wealth, indulging themselves in every luxury; then just as suddenly, they could be completely broke, living in the dire straits of abject poverty. According to the saying, "Wealth does not last for more than three generations." *The Connected Discourses of the Buddha* also points out, that "all phenomena are impermanent;" And over the centuries, few of the imperial dynasties of China lasted for more than six emperors. Moreover, the wealthy nobility under the many dynasties all ended in downfall. And on the other hand, many of the very wealthy people and learned scholars came from very poor families. Therefore, the honor, disgrace, wealth, and poverty in this world are all impermanent. Though we may be down and out for the moment, as long as we are willing to work hard and persevere, we will surely succeed one day.

4. In cultivation, the Buddha and our demons are half and

half. This is the world where the Buddha and our demons are present together and where misfortune and fortune exist at the same time. Living in this half-and-half world, there is the world of the Buddha and that of our demons. In reality, they exist between our thoughts, for when we can turn our thinking around, we can change ignorance into enlightenment, sorrow into joy, stupidity into wisdom, and harmful thoughts into compassion. As the saying goes, "Put down the butcher's knife and become a Buddha right here and now." Therefore, within the half-and-half world of the Buddha and our demons, we can transform the demonic into the Buddha, enabling us to become virtuous and wise.

The world is divided in half between good and bad. Most people can only accept the good half and not the bad. As a result, they can only achieve half of what they have set out to do. We can possess a complete life only when we can accept the good half and tolerate the bad half as well. Therefore, we need to understand clearly this half-and-half life of ours.

Wondrous Causes and Effects

"The arising of all phenomena depends on external conditions; no phenomenon is caused by itself." No event or thing in this world can exist by itself without causes and conditions. No existence is accidental or non-contingent. The saying, "Such is the cause and such is the effect," tells us that the cause of a wondrous effect is itself wondrous. The following examples illustrate the wonders of causes and effects:

1. Calmness leads to enlightenment. While it is the wish of everyone to be wise and insightful, how can we transform our knowledge, experience, and realizations into wisdom? According to the sutras, "Bodhisattvas frequently traverse the ultimate emptiness under the pure moon. Enlightenment will manifest itself in the minds of those who are without delusion." In order for the river to clearly reflect the moon, the water must be calm and clear. Often, people are capable of recalling their past and remembering what they have forgotten when their minds are at peace and without delusion. Therefore, Buddhism talks about ethics, meditative contemplation, and wisdom. Wisdom is born through the practice of insightful meditation, and so calmness is one of the wondrous causes of enlightenment.

2. Practice leads to perfection. "The first step of every task is always the hardest," but once we have acquired the necessary skills, we will have little trouble in becoming an expert. For instance, in learning how to ride a bike, swim, play a musical instrument, or use the computer, practice makes perfect. The same goes for reading a book, where careful reading of the words brings a clear understanding of the text and helps us remember their

meaning in our daily lives. It is like what poet Su Shi said, "A book can be read again and again tirelessly by a scholar who knows that painstaking effort is the only way for him to have a deep understanding." Therefore, practice is the wondrous cause of perfection.

3. Diligence leads to achievement. According to the commentary on the *Spring and Autumn Annals* [*Zuoshi Chun Qiu*], "People's livelihood depends on diligence." As long as there is diligence, there is no poverty; and as long as there is hard work, there is no failure. The same applies to learning, for with diligence we can gain knowledge. Therefore, hard work produces wealth, and diligence brings knowledge. Beethoven said, "Mastery is only possible by means of persistent hard work." For any situation in the world, diligence is the key to success and hard work the means to riches. Therefore, diligence is the wondrous cause of achievement.

4. Joy leads to happiness. If we can be happy every day of our lives with the people we see and the things we do, we will be like the monk Budai who laughed away all the world's sorrows with his happiness, spreading joy to every living being. Happiness is like a candle that brings light once lit, or like the rays of the sun cutting through and melting away what is cold and frozen. The famous Tang poet Bai Juyi once remarked, "Only the ignorant do not laugh." We need to have joy in our hearts all the time so that life will be happy, and our interpersonal relationships will achieve harmony. Therefore, joy is the wondrous cause of happiness.

As the saying goes, "one reaps what one sows." This is echoed by Dr. Hu Shi who said, "Our rewards depend on our efforts."

GLOSSARY

Amitabha Buddha: The Buddha of the Western Pure Land, also known as the Buddha of Infinite Light. Amitabha Buddha is described as vowing to purify a realm for those who desire to seek rebirth there by earnestly reciting his name. Sometimes known as Amita Buddha or Amitayus Buddha (the Buddha of Infinite Life.)

Avalokitesvara Bodhisattva: The Bodhisattva of Compassion who can manifest in any conceivable form to bring help to those in need. In China, Avalokitesvara Bodhisattva is usually portrayed in a female form, and also known as the Bodhisattva "Guanyin."

Bodhi: "Awakened" or "enlightened." In the state of *bodhi*, one is awakened to one's own Buddha Nature, having eliminated all afflictions and delusions, and achieved prajna-wisdom.

Bodhisattva: An enlightened being. It is a compound word made up of "*bodhi*" and "*sattva*." *Bodhi* means "enlightened" and *sattva* means "being." Therefore, the term *bodhisattva* refers to a being that has attained enlightenment through practicing all six *paramitas*. Bodhisattvas vow to remain in the world, postponing their own full enlightenment by entering nirvana, in order to liberate all beings. The *bodhisattva* ideal is the defining feature of Mahayana Buddhism.

Buddha: Literally "The awakened one." Used as a generic term to refer to one who has achieved enlightenment and attained complete liberation from the cycle of existence (see *samsara*). More commonly used to refer to the Sakyamuni Buddha, the historical founder of Buddhism (581-501 B.C.E.). He was born the prince of Kapilavastu and the son of King Suddhodana. At the age of twenty-nine, he left the royal palace and his family to search for the meaning of existence. Six years later, he attained enlightenment under the Bodhi tree. He then spent the next forty-five years expounding his teachings, which include the Four Noble Truths, the Noble Eightfold Path, the Law of Cause and Effect, and the Twelve Links of Dependent Origination. At the age of eighty, he entered the state of *parinirvana.*

Buddha Nature: The true nature or inherent potential for achieving Buddhahood that exists in all beings.

Chan: A school of Buddhism that emphasizes enlightenment through deep concentration, meditation, and internal cultivation. Practicing Chan Buddhism does not rely upon intellectual reasoning, analysis of doctrine, or academic studies, but instead, relies upon a profound inner concentration that can reveal and illuminate one's true nature. (The term is pronounced "Zen" in Japanese.)

Dharma: Literally "that which is preserved or maintained." Usually refers to the teachings of the Buddha. When capitalized, it means: 1) the ultimate truth and 2) the teachings of the Buddha. When the Dharma is applied or practiced in life it is referred to as: 3) righteousness or virtue. When it appears with a lowercase "d" it means: 4) anything that can be thought of, experienced, or named; close in meaning to the word "phenomena."

Five Aggregates: Indicating form, feelings, perceptions, mental formation, and consciousness, which together and *interdependently* constitute what we commonly regard as an "individual personality." Also known as the "*five skandhas.*"

Five Contemplations for Eating: Five contemplations of which practitioners should be mindful when they take their meals. They include being grateful for the effort in producing and making the food; making sure one's heart and mind is pure and deserving of the offering; guarding oneself against greed in consuming the food;

treating the food as medicine to nourish the body; and accepting the food as sustenance on the path of spiritual cultivation.

Five Precepts: Guiding principles in Buddhism that teach proper conduct. These are: 1) no killing, 2) no stealing, 3) no sexual misconduct, 4) no lying, and 5) no taking of intoxicating substances.

Four Elements: In Buddhism, all matters are composed of the elements of earth, water, fire, and wind.

Four Immeasurables: This refers to: 1) the state of boundless loving-kindness in giving others happiness; 2) the state of boundless compassion in liberating others from suffering; 3) the state of boundless joyfulness in keeping others away from suffering; 4) the state of boundless equanimity in treating others equally and without discrimination.

Four Noble Truths: One of the most fundamental Buddhist teachings about the nature and existence of suffering: 1) the truth of suffering, 2) the truth of the cause of suffering, 3) the truth of cessation of suffering, and 4) the truth of the path leading to the cessation of suffering.

Guanyin: Popular Chinese reference to Avalokitesvara Bodhisattva.

Humanistic Buddhism: The primary teaching of the Venerable Master Hsing Yun, which emphasizes putting Buddhism into practice in our daily life, and building a pure land in this human world.

Kalpa: A unit of temporal measurement used in ancient India, that signifies an immense and inconceivable length of time. Buddhism adapted it to refer to the time between the creation and re-creation of worlds.

Karma: Defined as "work, action, or deeds" and is related to the Law of Cause and Effect. All mental, verbal, and physical deeds that are governed by *intention*, both good or bad, produce effects. The effects may be experienced instantly, or they may accumulate and not come into fruition for many years or even many lifetimes.

Law of Cause and Condition: A universal truth in Buddhism based on the dependent origination of all phenomena in primary causes and secondary causes (conditions). The seed out of which a plant or a flower grows is a good illustration of a primary cause. The elements of soil, water, sunlight could be considered the necessary conditions for growth.

Law of Cause and Effect: This is the most basic doctrine in Buddhism, which explains the formation of all relations and connections in the world. This law shows that the arising of each and every phenomenon is due to its own causes and conditions, while the actual form, or manifestation, of all phenomena is the effect.

Mahayana: Literally, "The Great Vehicle," referring to one of the two main traditions of Buddhism, the other being Theravada. Mahayana Buddhism stresses that helping all sentient beings attain enlightenment is more important than just self-liberation.

Nirvana: Literally "extinction," but also can mean "calmed, quieted, tamed, or ceasing." In Buddhism, it refers to the absolute extinction of individual existence, or of all afflictions and desires; it is the state of liberation, beyond birth and death. It is also the final spiritual goal for all branches of Buddhism.

Noble Eightfold Path: Eight right ways leading to the cessation of suffering according to the Four Noble Truths as taught by the Buddha. They are: 1) right view; 2) right thought; 3) right speech; 4) right action; 5) right livelihood; 6) right effort; 7) right mindfulness; and 8) right concentration.

Prajna: Literally "consciousness" or "wisdom." As the highest form of wisdom, *prajna* is the wisdom of insight into "emptiness," which is the true nature of all phenomena. The realization of *prajna* also implies the attainment of enlightenment, and is in this sense one of the six *paramitas* or "perfections" of the *bodhisattva* path. Sometimes referred to by the compound term, *prajna-wisdom.*

Pure Land: Pure Land practice can be traced back to India and the teachings of the Buddha. It remains the most popular worldwide of all the 84,000 different Buddhist paths to supreme enlightenment. The Pure Land practitioner seeks rebirth in the Pure Land of Amitabha Buddha first through the cultivation of *bodhicitta*, or the aspiration for enlightenment; and second, through the practice of reciting the name of Amitabha Buddha with sincerity and deep devotion, and cultivating one's life through the three trainings of precepts, concentration, and *prajna*. Together, they enable one to more rapidly purify one's mind and liberate oneself from all delusions. Although one is not free from all wants and fears in the Pure Land, one is no longer bound by them. The Pure Land can also be found in this world with all its imperfections by the devout practitioner.

Samadhi: The highest state of mind achieved through meditation, chanting, reciting the Buddha's name, or other practices, in which the mind has reached ultimate concentration, so that it is no longer subject to thoughts and distractions. The highest state of *samadhi* is the "*bodhi*" or enlightened mind.

Sunyata: Literally "emptiness" or "void." This is a central concept in Buddhism, which asserts that everything existing in the world is due to dependent origination and has no permanent self or substance. Its meaning is twofold: 1) emptiness of living beings, which means that human beings or other living beings have no unchanging, substantial self; or 2) emptiness of *dharmas*, which means that the existence of all phenomena is due to causes and conditions. Unlike nihilism, this concept does not imply nothing exists, rather it stresses that all existence is without independent substance or absolute essence.

Sutra: Literally "threaded together." Refers to the scriptures taught directly by the Buddha and recorded by his disciples for all to follow in their practice. The direct assertion that these are the teachings of the Buddha is implied by the opening line of each sutra, "Thus have I heard."

Tathagata: Refers to one who has attained supreme enlightenment. The historical Sakyamuni Buddha used this title when speaking of himself or other Buddhas.

Ten Dharma Realms: These are the realms of: 1) hell, 2) hungry ghosts, 3) animals, 4) asuras, 5) humans, 6) heavens, 7) sravakas, 8) pratyekabuddhas, 9) bodhisattvas, and 10) Buddhas.

Ten Virtuous Practices: Buddhist teachings that instruct practitioners to: 1) protect and nurture life, 2) abstain from stealing, 3) abstain from sexual misconduct, 4) speak truthfully, 5) foster good relationships, 6) speak gently and use encouraging words, 7) speak sincerely, 8) practice generosity, 9) practice patience and tolerance, and 10) uphold the right view.

Theravada: Literally, "the teaching of the elders of the order" in Pali, referring to one of the eighteen schools during the Period of Sectarian Buddhism. Unlike the *bodhisattva* ideal in Mahayana tradition, this school's emphasis is on the liberation of the individual. In the 3rd century B.C.E., it was transmitted to Sri Lanka from India. Today it is popular in many areas of Southeast Asia.

About the Author

Venerable Master Hsing Yun

Founder of the Fo Guang Shan (Buddha's Light Mountain) Buddhist Order and the Buddha's Light International Association, Venerable Master Hsing Yun has dedicated his life to teaching Humanistic Buddhism, which seeks to realize spiritual cultivation in everyday living.

Master Hsing Yun is the 48th Patriarch of the Linji Chan School. Born in Jiangsu Province, China in 1927, he was tonsured under Venerable Master Zhikai at the age of twelve and became a novice monk at Qixia Vinaya College. He was fully ordained in 1941 following years of strict monastic training. When he left Jiaoshan Buddhist College at the age of twenty, he had studied for almost ten years in a monastery.

Due to the civil war in China, Master Hsing Yun moved to Taiwan in 1949 where he undertook the revitalization of Chinese Mahayana Buddhism. He began fulfilling his vow to promote the Dharma by starting chanting groups, student and youth groups, and other civic-minded organizations with Leiyin Temple in Ilan as his base. Since the founding of Fo Guang Shan monastery in Kaohsiung in 1967, more than two hundred temples have been established worldwide. Hsi Lai Temple, the symbolic torch of the Dharma spreading to the West, was built in 1988 near Los Angeles.

Master Hsing Yun has been guiding Buddhism on a course of modernization by integrating Buddhist values into education, cultural activities, charity, and religious practices. To achieve these ends, he travels all over the world, giving lectures and actively engaging in religious dialogue. The Fo Guang Shan organization also oversees sixteen Buddhist colleges and four universities, one of which is the University of the West in Rosemead, California.

Over the past fifty years, Master Hsing Yun has written many books teaching Humanistic Buddhism and defining its practice. Whether providing insight into Buddhist sutras, human nature, or inter-religious exchange, he stresses the need for respect, compassion, and tolerance among all beings in order to alleviate suffering in this world. His works have been translated into English, French, German, Japanese, Korean, Portuguese, Russian, Spanish, Sinhalese, and Thai.

About the Company

Buddha's Light Publishing
Fo Guang Shan International Translation Center

For as long as Venerable Master Hsing Yun has been a Buddhist monk, he has had a firm belief that books and other means of transmitting the Buddha's teachings can unite us spiritually, help us practice Buddhism at a higher altitude, and continuously challenge our views on how we define and live our lives.

In 1996, the Fo Guang Shan International Translation Center was established with this goal in mind. This marked the beginning of a series of publications translated into various languages from the Master's original writings in Chinese. Presently, several translation centers have been set up worldwide. Centers that coordinate translation or publication projects are located in Los Angeles, USA; Montreal, Canada; Sydney, Australia; Berlin, Germany; France; Sweden; Argentina; Brazil; South Africa; Japan; Korean; and Thailand.

In 2001, Buddha's Light Publishing was established to publish Buddhist books translated by Fo Guang Shan International Translation Center as well as other important Buddhist works. Buddha's Light Publishing is committed to building bridges between East and West, Buddhist communities, and cultures. All proceeds from our book sales support Buddhist propagation efforts.

Notes

Notes

Notes

Notes